EDUCATION FOR SUSTAINABLE DEVELOPMENT

Education for Sustainable Development

Edited by
Rajarshi Roy

SHIPRA

ISBN: 978-81-7541-743-4

First Published in India in 2014

Education for Sustainable Development

Published by:
SHIPRA PUBLICATIONS
H.O.: LG 18-19, Pankaj Central Market, Patparganj,
I.P. Ext., Delhi-110092, Tel: 91-11-2223 5152, 2223 6152
Br.Off.: 4617/18, Ansari Road, Darya Ganj,
New Delhi-110002, Tel: 9650028065, 9810522367
E-mail: info@shiprapublications.com
www.shiprapublications.com

Preface

The basic requirements for survival of any species are termed as 'propensities'. A list of human propensity includes *food, shelter, health* and *safety* (commonly known as survival needs/propensities), *education, employment* and at the present day, possibly the *various forms of agro and industrial development*, which, in the post modern society, shifted towards *development of information technology* and *knowledge-development* for the sake of maintaining life style (commonly known as developmental needs) and *security.*

Of course, man doesn't survive only on rice or bread. Human needs go beyond the purely physical aspects and are immersed in social and economic environment as well. We do require meaningful employment and job satisfaction, environment, leisure and some human qualities like respect, care and affection, etc. Deprived of these, a person may languish just as surely as if deprived of food and water.

Most of our physical needs demand access to natural resources such as *land, water* and *air*, which, with the aid of radiant energy from the sun, generate plants and animals. The so-called nonrenewable resource such as minerals and fossil-fucls, are also needed for human survival and development. All these resources are present on a thin layer of the earth's surface, which is commonly termed as *environment*. Actually it is the environment within which we live. Therefore, it is considerably clear that the link remains among the environment, human beings and, their needs.

On the other hand, technology is the applied field of science, which provides knowledge to satisfy human needs (*and sometimes, human greed too, at the cost of the environment*). Education, science and technology provide knowledge and thereby help the human beings to produce dramatic improvements to enrich human propensities and needs. Right now, we are in a landmark of human history, accompanied with enhanced intelligentsia and creativity, we are changing the basic components of our environment by adding synthetic and chemical products and by-products and thereby changing the *hydrosphere* and *atmosphere*.

There has been unprecedented growth in the awareness of the environment across the world, during the past four decades. The driving factors have been the concern for quality of life for the mankind. Developmental process and the resulting growth would remain meaningless unless they are suitably reinforced with focused efforts for the protection of environment. People are becoming increasingly conscious of varieties of problems like *global warming, ozone layer depletion, acid rain, famines, droughts, flood, scarcity of fuel, fire wood and fodder, pollution of air and water and problem from hazardous chemicals and radiation* which have adverse impact over the environment. Raising environmental awareness and gaining public participation and cooperation in actions leading to achievements of environmental goal selected has to be done through *environmental education* of the people, children, youth, adults and public workers. Education is the process through which man is trained for the society, in which he lives, and at the same time learns to realize his individual potential.

Education is a process of socialization that enables the young to achieve *adult standard of technical performances* and the capacity to take part in the social life of the extended family, the community and the country to which they belong. It is necessary that the standard should be—people are made to realize the enormity of the problem of environmental degradation.

Importance of sustainable development and maintenance of proper environment should be disseminated to the young and coming generations from the childhood itself. Environmental education should form a part of curriculum, even for the school going children.

Since the day of prehistory, there are regular technological developments to fulfill the needs of human being, such as food, shelter, and safety. Development in every sphere of human activity is an unending and continuous process. The modern world is witnessing tremendous progress in each and every field of science and technology such as in nuclear sciences, space sciences, electronic engineering, and biological sciences and so on, but at the same time there advancements are bringing about destruction and disasters in some quarters. This is due to thoughtless interference of man over environment, which has caused enormous damage to the environment not only for present time s/he lives in but also charring it for future generations. To meet the present crisis, the sustainability in development is the only solution. Need of the hour is that the students should be made to realize the enormity of the various environmental problems with minimum technicalities.

The popular definition of sustainable development is '...to meet the needs of the present without compromising the ability of the future generations to meet their own needs' as quoted in Brundtland Commission Report in 1987.

It is a fact that consideration of human needs presumes that human beings must actively seek ways to improve the quality of their life. This further reveals that education-irrespective of its content-areas is a value-loaded connotation. It is accepted without any doubt that improvement of social and economic status of the human beings is needed. Development must continue to be promoted in both industrialized and traditionally developed societies; however, there should be a balance between the utilization pattern of natural resources and economic growth. Economic and social development are always welcome, but not at the cost of renewable and non-renewable natural resources. Such forms of development, which considers the environment and its protection, must last on this planet for a long, long time if not ever, be termed as *sustainable development*. Increased support to environmental protection will ensure ecological balance and ultimately ensure sustainable development.

Environmental Education in India possesses a significant contribution from its history. Our epic *Isho Upanishad* said long ago, "*...this universe is the creation of the supreme power and is meant for the benefit of all; Individual species must therefore learn to enjoy its benefits by regarding themselves as a part of the system in close relationship with other species; therefore let not any one species encroach upon the right of others*."

These thoughts are represented in the rituals of the people of this land since the Indian civilization came into existence, and since then, our norms, customs values, mores, lore and over all, culture developed in such a way that follows the worship of nature and its various components, and thereby ensure preservation of the environment. However, this philosophy was attacked since the end of last century with the propagation of exotic-philosophies. As a result, the policy of education got boost from exotic agencies in such a way, which hindered the preservation of environmental resources. Being in Sanskrit, the *Upanishadic* thoughts have remained a close look far from us not only on account of the language barrier, but also due to lack of good environmental communicators among those who know the *Sanskrit language*.

Switching over from the perspective of Environmental Education, it is felt that time has come to have a look over our existing system of education at varied level and to twin the same with the concept of sustainable development.

Formal education, if be equated with 'bookish knowledge', better to say, 'theoretical knowledge', often exhibit a gap with the practice among the educated. In this venture, the volume on 'Education and sustainable development' is introduced to the reader to explore the future scope of exploring whether the education contributes for sustainable development in reality or not. Also the connotation 'Education and sustainable development', as comprehended by various contributors be understood, which is expected to generate a new branch, differing from 'Environmental Education' within the domain of Education in coming days.

Rajarshi Roy

Contents

1

An Ecosystemic Approach to Improve Educational Systems

Alberto Arenas

In restructuring educational systems, strategies are put into place that address different aspects of education, but too often these reforms are fragmented and not part of a larger framework for understanding the system as a whole. Consequently, changes end up as a hotchpotch of practices that do not sustain, and regularly contradict, each other. This chapter proposes the overall framework of an eco-systemic approach for analyzing and revamping social systems in general, and educational systems in particular.

'Ecosystem' will be used as a root metaphor. According to C.A. Bowers (1993), root or generative metaphors provide a basic conceptual template that helps individuals make sense of the world around them. Given the metaphorical nature of language, root metaphors inevitably influence the way people interpret their experiences. Throughout the twentieth century, the dominant root metaphor for schools has been that of machines; schools are viewed as possessing interchangeable, disposable, lifeless parts with individuals whose actions can be standardized, manipulated, and controlled. When the root metaphor of an ecosystem is employed, the school is perceived as an entity that is alive, with interdependent relationships that need support and nourishment. The school is then considered as an entity of interacting elements that form a single totality through a complex exchange of people, matter, energy, and information.

In order to expound on the parallelisms between education and ecology, concepts are borrowed from Gregory Bateson (1972), the Center for Eco-literacy (formerly the Elmwood Institute, 1993) and John and Nancy Todd (1984). Bateson's use of 'ecology' allows for the creation of a metaphorical framework that places the individual and its institutions in a system of interdependent relations between culture and nature. In this context, ecological principles are applied to the way schools and educational systems can be re-organized as learning communities. Schools are not viewed as physical places but as processes. All members are seen as linked in a web of relationships that place the individual, the community and the ecosystem as part of the same organic whole.

Does Nature Know Best?

While the idea of finding inspiration in the principles of nature to design modern complex human systems such as cities, neighborhoods, farms, and schools is of relatively recent development. The concept of using nature as a model of design has existed since time immemorial from indigenous groups engaging in polycultures with multiple crops in the same space. Leonardo da Vinci, was a key advocate of using nature as a mode for design—his sketchbooks are filled with inventions that closely mimic the operations of nature—to the modern field of biomimicry, which addresses human needs by imitating or taking inspiration from the systems, processes, and elements of nature (Benyus, 1997). John and Nancy Todd (1984) proposed nine principles to help them design everything from less complex systems such as a house to a more complex one such an economic system. These principles are:

1. The living world is the matrix of all design
2. Design should follow the laws of nature
3. Biological equity must determine design
4. Design must reflect bio-regionality
5. Projects should be based on renewable energy sources
6. Design should integrate living systems
7. Design should be co-evolutionary
8. Building and design should heal the planet
9. Design should follow a sacred ecology

A related approach of using nature as a model of design is the one proposed by Fritjoj Capra (2005) and the Center for Eco-literacy. Here the focus is on applying systems thinking to the relationships interlinking members in ecosystems and across ecosystems to describe the patterns and processes that sustain life. Capra and associates have identified eight principles to bring about sustainable societies, which, as the author stated at the beginning of this chapter, more closely resembles the principles used in this work:

1. Networks

2. Nested systems
3. Interdependence
4. Diversity
5. Cycles
6. Flows
7. Development
8. Dynamic Balance

The idea of establishing parallels between ecosystems and social systems has been called into question by some scholars (e.g., Dryzek, 1987). They base their opposition on three main arguments: first, human groups have culture and with it a sense of what is right and wrong, good and bad, fair and unjust. In ecosystems there are no such equivalents and any such equivalency would corrupt the meaning of these cultural traits. Second, a danger of following nature too closely may lead to wholesale ecological engineering, the creation of a 'noosphere,' a totally artificial environment through which humans transcend nature. In this scenario, valuable cultural practices that emerge or are sustained over time independently of the environment would be sub-ordinated to ecology's dicta. And third, it is too pessimistic to advocate a minimum of human intervention in natural systems. This would preclude the possibility of creating what has been called "an anthropogenic sub-climax" (Dryzek, 1987, p. 45), a stable ecological state that serves the needs of human communities while protecting the integrity of the surrounding ecosystem.

In general, while each of these arguments is correct, it is possible to engage in a social design along ecological principles without falling prey to any one of these problems. Using nature as a guiding metaphor does not negate the importance of culture or the influence that culture has on the environment. Just as cultures vary from place to place, so do ecosystems. A reasonable ecological model should be sensitive to these differences and to the co-evolutionary development of both. Also, one does not need to go to any extremes of environmental determinism (humans as slaves of nature or masters of nature) to apply the teachings of nature for improving social institutions. Finally, the attitude of maximum intervention in the environment can be replaced by one of sufficient intervention without adopting a dismal outlook on the future. Prudence and frugality need not be synonymous with pessimism and pauperism. An ecological model for social design seeks precisely to reach anthropogenic sub-climaxes, many of which heed closely to ecological considerations (e.g., aquaculture systems in East Asia that integrate production and waste-elimination processes).

Several reasons lead to the conclusion that social systems ought to be structurally and epistemologically organized around the most current understanding of eco-systemic behaviour. First, all social systems are an integral part of, and completely dependent upon, the biosphere. Ecosystems are vivid examples of millions of years of gradual evolutionary change. When an ecosystem is threatened by external disruptions, its resilience to adapt may be greatly diminished. The lesson here is for humans to learn to live gracefully within the environmental confines imposed by every ecosystem. Since ecosystems are the only systems humans know of that maintain stability and protect its members over a long period of time, it makes sense to use ecosystems as a guiding metaphor (Commoner, 1992).

Second, nature is a part of us, just as we are a part of nature. We are intimately connected to the land that supports us, and as such have an ethical responsibility towards safeguarding its welfare (Leopold, 1971). What better way of protecting it than by following the elegant and simple lessons that all healthy ecosystems contain?

Third, ecology is not just another scientific discipline but rather a unified science. The biosphere and all its constituent parts cannot be understood fully in terms of the arbitrary divisions to which knowledge has been subject. Ecology is a synthetic discipline essential to increasing our understanding of the structure and function of the biosphere, and hence it can provide the framework for understanding the other disciplines and their objects of study (Goldsmith, 1993).

The fourth and last reason is based on spirituality (Cobb, 1994). John Cobb states that all living entities, including the associations they create, should be viewed as constituting a set of relations with the rest of the world. Human experience can only be fully understood in its multiple relationships with non-human beings. A spiritual approach would view the ecological model as comprising the totality of relations that are perfect and complementary.

Relating Ecosystems to Educational Systems

Ecosystems function according to a set of principles. Each ecologist has a favourite list of principles that he or she believes best characterizes a system. This list is determined by each scientist's own projection on how she or he thinks an ecosystem functions, just like the two lists mentioned above by John and Nancy Todd (1984) and Capra (2005). In the early 1990s the British Ecological Society surveyed its members regarding the ten most important principles of ecology (Hale, 1993). The result was a lengthy list of 50 concepts. From this unwieldy number there were six principles that most consistently showed up in most of the lists: Interdependence; energy and matter flows; carrying capacity; diversity; resilience; and relationships. Although for didactic purposes each principle is treated as a separate category, they are all linked and should be seen as part of a web in which all the strands are connected and complementary. It is the combination of principles in a web-like structure that ultimately determines the sustainability of a system over time.

After describing each ecological principle, examples are provided as to their application in education. The examples provided are not intended to be exhaustive; rather, they intend to give a preliminary appreciation as to the usefulness of this approach.

Interdependence

The cardinal principle in ecology, interdependence, brings unity to members in a community. In an ecosystem, the health of the whole depends upon the health of each element, just as much as the health of each element depends upon that of the whole. As a result, despite an organism's partial autonomy, no organism can survive on its own.

In the modern school, one group of actors is dependent on one another, but little meaningful *inter*-dependence exists. Students are wholly dependent on the teacher from whom they receive knowledge, guidance, instructions, and sanctioning. Teachers in turn are dependent to a high degree on the administration for guidelines, curricula, scheduling and promotion. Administrators are dependent on the central office for funding, in-house training, testing materials and personnel hiring. In sum, the modern school is a ladder of hierarchies in which those in sub-ordinated positions are the constant recipients of decisions and actions from above.

In contrast, an ecosystemic approach views every member as dependent on each other in a multi-directional web of relationships. Ultimately, it is expected that individuals will get to know each other beyond the narrow unidimensional function that the modern school has assigned to them. Students rely on the teacher for guidance, just as much as the teacher needs students for new ideas, clarity, and a sense of accomplishment. The teacher counts on the administration for guidelines, just as the administration builds upon the teacher's input to improve its organization and efficiency. The teacher invites community members to share their knowledge to enrich the curriculum, just as the community pins its faith on the school to assist in the formation of wholesome individuals.

The need for a reciprocal connection goes beyond interactions between the different constituencies. Other areas of mutual connection include an interdisciplinary curriculum, the combination of intellectual activities with manual ones, studying inside and outside the school, and allowing the student to see that he or she is an inseparable part of the surroundings.

Energy and Matter Flows

Ecosystems are open systems that require the constant flow of energy and the recycling of matter. Energy enters an ecosystem in the form of solar energy and matter enters, among other forms, as water and carbon dioxide. The flow of matter and energy takes place through numerous pathways, in accordance with the food choices available to each organism. An important aspect of this food web is the absence of "waste": all matter is continuously recycled in the system. What for one element is refuse for another is a feast, as in the case of manure decomposed by microorganisms.

This principle is painfully omitted from modern schools. The campus is not seen as a legitimate object of study and thus is treated as a black box. Students seldom learn about the sources of energy and matter that enter the campus (e.g., electricity, water, paper, books) or the eventual deposits of the organic waste and garbage that leaves the campus. The black box treatment is also seen in the physical and epistemological precipice that separates the school from the community. A century ago John Dewey expressed this sentiment when he wrote (in McDermott, 1973),

> 'The school has been so set apart, so isolated from ordinary conditions and motives of life, that the place where children are sent—is the one place in the world where it is most difficult to get experience.'

The ecological school, in contrast, is surrounded by a permeable membrane that allows the permanent inflow and outflow between the school and the community. The bioregion becomes a giant school and every aspect of it becomes an integral part of the curriculum. Given that new knowledge and skills are required, students and teachers learn *together*, challenging the basic practice of the omniscient-teacher. Other advantages involve leaving the campus to learn in real contexts, interacting with community members, and expanding one's sense of responsibility and belongingness. Pertinent to waste is that schools must learn to consider garbage as a potential resource. It is up to students, teachers and other members of the learning community to recast this concentrated ore into a worthwhile, and perhaps even profitable, output. These elements together create what has been called pedagogy of place, which is established to help students think, feel and behave as part of a larger web of life and grounded in the bioregion inhabited by the students (Orr, 1992).

Carrying Capacity

Carrying capacity is the maximum number of organisms that can be adequately supported by an ecosystem for an indefinite period of time. When a population grows faster than the availability of resources in an area, a protective mechanism becomes activated that reduces the fertility rate and increases the age of first reproduction (Kirk, 1975). This ensures enough resources for the various species in the area.

Large numbers of students endure crowded classrooms since the inception of the modern school. This reality has changed little over the decades as it is common for a teacher to head a class of 30 or more students. Moreover, campuses teem with hundreds and even thousands of students. These overflowing institutions have an unmistakable financial logic: money is saved on teacher salaries and other costs associated with running more schools. However, too high a social price has been paid for this giantism. Students have been left alienated, anonymous, and excluded from the learning process.

Educational research has focused on the relationship between class size and student achievement. Earlier scholarship argued that reducing class size had little or no positive effect on student performance (e.g., Hanushek, 1996; Odden, 1990). More recent studies however showed that these earlier works mistakenly used pupil-teacher ratio (PTR) as equivalent to class size (Achilles, 1998; ED/OERI, 1998). PTR is an average that does not reflect the actual number of students in a given class. When studies account for actual class size, students do in fact gain from class-size reduction, especially minority and at-risk students.

The concept of carrying capacity as applied to the modern school is best understood when compared to pre-modern means of rearing children (Smith, 1992). Given that each child had several adults or older children to care for them, close interaction was the norm, not the exception. Children learned side by side with their parents and other relatives. They observed and imitated activities that were concrete and rooted in their daily life. Feedback was received almost immediately. Through their active participation, children felt engaged in and contributors to the well-being of the family and community. Without romanticizing pre-industrial life, it would seem that the potential for alienation and anonymity is much greater in modern societies than in ones where intimate relationships among community members are the norm.

For an ecological school, the lessons are obvious: cut down on the number of students per classroom and school, and increase the number of adults who can serve as mentors (a viable alternative are schools within schools). While in the short run expenses may be greater, in the long run money is saved. Societies will pay less in devastating social costs, leading to fewer prisons, drug and alcohol rehabilitation centers, homeless shelters, and so on. These enormous social problems are certainly not directly caused by overcrowded classrooms, but it stands to reason that if children spend at least 13 years of their life in a situation of virtual anonymity, the cumulative side effects must be felt down the road in full.

Diversity

Diversity is the number of species that inhabit an ecosystem. When a severe disturbance affects an ecosystem, a species-rich ecosystem will be far stronger over time than a species-poor one (Baskin, 1997). When an external force, such as a tornado, hits an ecosystem, the whole needs to modify to compensate for the disturbance. A species-poor community is affected more in the long run because it has fewer species to adapt to the new changes. As Baskin (1997) wrote, in a diverse ecosystem,

> 'When the work of one of the species is hampered by drought or other conditions, another species—is likely to thrive and expand its activities. It is this ability of species to compensate for one another that allows the system as a whole to function steadily over the long term.'

The main threat to diversity is seen in the homogenization of educational systems around the world. The layout of a campus, the bureaucratic structure, the division of time, the forms of pedagogy and testing, are all greatly uniformed regardless of region or country (Fuller, 1991; Boli *et al.,* 1985). Both in terms of content and form, the modern school continues to legitimize only a very narrow set of cultural behaviours and beliefs. Local cultures and particularistic visions of the world are neglected and ignored.

At the K-12 level, diversity has been limited in schools to a more accurate examination of history and to the celebration of annual ethnic festivals. While this is important, a diverse education must also delve deeply into other groups' mythologies, values, and practices. The study of their kinship relationships, gender roles, birth and death rituals and sources of authority would allow students and teachers to reach beneath superficial cultural layers, and arrive more closely to a truly diverse curriculum. Other changes include: scientific, objective knowledge is complemented with non-rational, artistic, and intuitive forms of knowing; the classroom ceases to be the privileged site for learning and becomes one among many sites; teachers and adults from the community collaborate in providing different perspectives on relevant issues; and several means for evaluating students' progress are employed.

Resilience

Resilience is the ability of an ecosystem to withstand internal or external pressures without instilling undue damage or deterioration to its normal functioning. If a part of an ecosystem is disrupted, it will affect other parts of the system as well. Below a certain threshold, feedback mechanisms "inform" the ecosystem of the disturbance and allow the system to return to a natural balance. As Janine Benyus (1997, p. 274) wrote,

> 'What makes a mature community runs is not one universal message being broadcasted from above, but numerous, even redundant messages coming from the grassroots, dispersed throughout the community structure. A rich feedback system allows changes in one component of the community to reverberate through the whole, allowing for adaptation when the environment changes.'

Transforming educational systems into less bureaucratic, less centralized, and less inflexible systems has been a concern for nations worldwide since the early 1980s (Fiske, 1996). Although reasons for educational decentralization vary from country to country, they generally include a political component (achieving stability and legitimacy for the central and local governments and increasing popular participation) and a technical one (improving the quality of education in terms of access and standards). While the road towards decentralization has not been free of obstacles, the process has alleviated the paralyzing inertia so common of giant bureaucracies. At the very least there has been an effort by school districts and individual institutions to include more public participation and to provide individualized answers to unique problems. A deepening of the decentralization process and a faithful reading of the resilience principle would mean full engagement in political decentralization. For an educational system to remain responsive and flexible, those directly affected at the local level must have real power to affect change.

Relationships

Species are connected to one another in numerous ways. Contrary to popular belief, competition and hierarchy play minor roles in these associations, and cooperation and egalitarianism appear to be more common and transcendental (Goldsmith, 1993). As Daniel Simberloff wrote, in natural habitats,

> 'it is rare to see two animals, particularly animals of different species, tugging at the same piece of meat. And even when competition is observed, it often appears inconsequential. Perhaps a fiddler crab scurries into a hole on a beach only to come running out again, expelled by the current inhabitant. But the crab simply moves off to find another hole. Competition between species thus appears to be little more than a minor, temporary inconvenience' (in Augrus and Stanciu, 1988, pp. 89-90).

Species also evolve mechanisms to avoid both intra-species and inter-species competition. Territoriality, hunting at different times of the day, growing up only to a certain size, periodic migrations, and dividing the same habitat into different niches are a few examples of strategies used to minimize the competition of limited resources. Lynn Margulis has even hypothesized that cooperative mechanisms are so important in nature that without them the evolution of beings larger than bacteria would have never taken place (Margulis and Sagan, 1995).

Relationships in the modern school are first and foremost competitive, hierarchical, and individualized. These practices go against a large body of literature that has emphasized repeatedly that knowledge transmission is acquired best through egalitarian practices, and that knowledge itself emerges from the interaction between members of a given community (e.g., Bosworth and Hamilton, 1994; Lave and Wenger, 1991). Schools thus neglect the fact that the most pressing economic, social, political and environmental problems cannot be solved by single individuals but by people working in close association.

Many teachers do try to establish collective work in their classrooms but few provide students with the necessary training. Consequently, students leave the classroom frustrated with group work and prefer to work individually. Yamane (1996) pointed out however that this can be avoided by careful selection of small groups, assigning specific responsibilities to members, and closely monitoring research teams.

The search for collective answers does not imply that individual work should be given up. Many writers know that long hours of solitude can result in profound and revolutionary insights. Likewise, this is true with competition. A modicum amount of competition can push students to excel in areas where they may otherwise become stagnant. An ecosystemic approach searches for the dynamic interplay between these opposites, while still using cooperation as the main foundation upon which the educational edifice is built.

Conclusion: The Limits of Metaphors

Metaphors are used to explain a new phenomenon in terms of a recognizable construct, or to obtain a fresh perspective on a familiar situation. The current metaphors applied to education too often show a mechanistic and technocratic approach to solving its problems: students are viewed as clients or customers, the process of learning as a set of inputs and outputs, and the outcome as cohorts of efficient and competitive graduates. This chapter has tried to show that when completely different root metaphors are used, the relationship and understanding that students, teachers, parents, and administrators have towards the institution will also be different.

Nonetheless, the application of ecological principles to social systems should not be interpreted in a narrow sense. Culture, what makes us human, is obviously absent in an ecosystem and a literal interpretation of ecosystemic thinking would cause more harm than good. A more liberal rendering of nature's lessons may provide missing clues as to how best to restructure societies and their relationship with the environment. It should be kept in mind however that using nature as a metaphor implies an interpretation as to how the cultural group considers nature to behave. Whatever 'lessons' are derived from nature are mediated through the prism of culture. Herein lies a crucial paradox. The modern scientific paradigm that is partly responsible for the mechanistic and reductionistic view of the world is also responsible for providing the ecological principles used to dismantle this same view. Perhaps this irony should be viewed as one of the many contradictions of modernity. In any case, the ecological model does provide us with perhaps the main principle that is absent in the classical, mechanical science: interdependence. Its understanding and application should be kept in mind when improving any social design in the field of education.

Another important lesson of using ecosystems as a metaphor is, just as there are no two ecosystems that are identical, no two educational systems should be identical either—which is anathema in the modern educational context. An ecosystem is formed out of a particular combination of living and non-living beings found in a given geographical area; cultures that emerge in those places are by nature different from other groups. This does not mean that individuals living in different parts of the world cannot learn from each other and adopt strategies and mechanisms that worked well elsewhere. But it does mean that social systems, including educational systems, must emerge from local knowledge and practices that have the pattern of place predicated upon them, and must create spaces that address the material, emotional, and spiritual needs of particular communities.

This article has sought to make the case that it is highly pertinent to use the language of nature as a metaphor for promoting sustainability, and to model societies and one of its institutions, schools, after the principles of ecology. Ecosystems are the result of millions of years of trail and error, and while they do not possess any human attributes such as fairness and solidarity, they do display a system of principles that tend to guarantee the survival of the various species that comprise the ecosystem. These principles of ecology, which may also be considered principles of sustainability or community, constitute the basic patterns that sustain life.

REFERENCES

Achilles, C.M. (1998). *Small-class Research Supports What We All Know (So, Why Aren't We Doing It?).* Paper presented at the Annual Meeting of the American Association of School Administrators, San Diego, California.

Augros, R., and Stanciu, G. (1988). *The New Biology: Discovering the Wisdom in Nature.* Boston: Shambala, New Science Library.

Baskin, I. (1997). *The Work of Nature: How the Diversity of Life Sustains Us.* Washington, D.C.: Island Press.

Bateson, G. (1972). *Steps to an Ecology of Mind.* New York: Ballentine.

Benyus, J.M. (1997). *Biomimicry: Innovation Inspired by Nature.* New York: William Marrow and Company, Inc.

Boli, J., Ramirez, F.O., and Meyer, J.W. (1985). Explaining the Origins and Expansion of Mass Education. *Comparative Education Review* 29(2), 145-170.

Bosworth, K. and Hamilton, S.J. (Eds.). (1994). *Collaborative Learning: Underlying Processes and Effective Techniques.* 59, Fall. San Francisco: Jossey-Bass Publishers.

Bowers, C.A. (1993). *Education, Cultural Myths, and the Ecological Crisis: Toward Deep Changes.* Albany: State University of New York.

Capra, F. (2005). Speaking nature's language: Principles of sustainability. In M. Stone and Z. Barlow (eds.), *Ecological Literacy: Educating our Children for a Sustainable World* (pp. 18-29). San Francisco: Sierra Club Books.

Cobb, J. Jr. (1994). Ecology and Process Theology. In Carolyn Merchant (ed.) *Ecology.* New Jersey: Humanities Press.

Commoner, B. (1992). *Making Peace With the Planet.* New York: The New Press.

Dryzek, J.S. (1987). *Rational Ecology: Environment and Political Economy.* Oxford: Basil Blackwell.

ED/OERI. (1998). *Reducing class size: What do we know.* Washington, D.C.: National Institute on Student Achievement, Curriculum and Assessment, Department of Education.

Elmwood Institute. (1993). Principles of Ecology-Principles of Education. *Guide to Eco-literacy.* Berkeley, California.

Fiske, E.B. (1996). *Decentralization in Education: Politics and Consensus.* Washington, D.C.: The World Bank.

Fuller, B. (1991). *Growing-Up Modern: The Western State Builds Third World Schools.* New York: Routledge.

Goldsmith, E. (1993). *The Way: An Ecological World-view.* Boston: Shambala Publications, Inc.

Hale, M. (Ed.). (1993). *Ecology in Education.* Cambridge, Massachusetts: Cambridge University Press.

Hanushek, E.A. (1996). A More Complete Picture of School Resource Policies. *Review of Educational Research,* 66 (3), 397-409.

Kirk, D. (Ed.). (1975). *Biology Today.* New York: Random House.

Lave, J. and Wenger, E. (1991). *Situated Learning: Legitimate peripheral participation.* Cambridge, England: Cambridge University Press.

Leopold, A. (1971). *A Sand County Almanac.* New York: Oxford University Press.

Margulis, L. and Sagan, D. (1995). *What is Life?* New York: Simon and Schuster.

McDermott, J.J. (Ed.). (1973). *The Philosophy of John Dewey: The Lived Experience* (Vol. 2). New York: G.P. Putnam's Sons.

Odden, A. (1990). Class Size and Student Achievement: Research-Based Policy Alternatives. *Educational Evaluation and Policy Analysis,* 12 (2), 213-227.

Orr, D.W. (2002). *The Nature of Design: Ecology, Culture, and the Human Intention.* Oxford, England: Oxford University Press.

Orr, D.W. (1992). *Ecological Literacy: Education and the Transition to a Postmodern World.* Albany: State University of New York Press.

Smith, G.A. (1992). *Education and the Environment: Learning to Live with Limits.* Albany: State University of New York Press.

Todd, J., and Todd, N. (1984). *Bioshelters, Ocean Arks, City Farming: Ecology as the Basis of Design.* San Francisco: Sierra Club Books.

Yamane, D. (1996). Collaboration and Its Discontents: Steps Toward Overcoming Barriers to Successful Group Projects. *Teaching Sociology,* 24 (4), 378-83.

2

Science, Technology and Teaching

Sensitivity for Sustainability and Non-Violation

Jayanti Basu

The chapter addresses the issue of developing concern for sustainability among the students of Science from the Higher Secondary level and the technical students. The traditional methods of teaching of science and technologies are being accused of knowingly or unknowingly inculcating violence on nature or violating human dignity. Therefore, a pedagogical paradigm shift in actual classroom teaching of science and technology needs to be evolved. Laws pertaining to the preservation of environment and impact on human health must be emphasized in the curriculum. However, actual change may be brought about only if the motivation for sustainable and eco-friendly innovation is promoted in the student community. Here the role of value education comes to achieve a position of prominence. In the present paper it is argued that innovative technical designing with eco-sensitivity in mind requires effective use of individualized learning, as well as training for a re-allocation of memory, attention, problem solving modes and decision making, not hereto tapped in traditional teaching-learning process. Ability for profitable yet non-violating decision making may require a specific kind of skill, or perhaps a flexible use of the executive function of the brain. Such skills have been used intuitively by a handful of creative persons, but not explored and understood enough to be put to use for changing the spirit of the curricula for technical education. Down-to-earth plans need to be forwarded for innovative research design in cognitive exploration to help modify the pedagogic challenges in science and technical education.

Sustainability in the context of teaching in science and technology is a theme of current and recurrent concern. The potentials of violation of nature and human dignity by technological innovations have long been a matter of politico-philosophical discourse (see the example of The Tao of Physics by Fritj of Capra, Science, hegemony and violence: A requiem for modernity, 1988, edited by Ashis Nandy or Brian Martin's paper in the Encyclopedia of Violence, Peace, and Conflict edited by Kurtz, 1999). This struggle over the past few decades has driven home the significance of consideration about sustainable development in science and technology practice.

Science or products of science are often naively considered as neutral. Science is not neutral of values, rather it is strongly value laden. Science provides us a methodology for living our life, and more importantly, provides a value system for adjudicating right and wrong, rational and irrational, enlightenment and superstition. Concepts and actions endorsed by 'science' are evaluated by common people as progressive and correct. Contrarily a piece of literature may be aesthetically pleasing to the reader, but may be perceived as imaginary and invalid in real world terms. Considering the social and moral authority science has on our daily lives, particularly when science is translated as intervention in terms of technology, the responsibility of science and technology teaching is morally huge. This entails not only knowing very clearly what good things we can do with technology, but also what good things we cannot do, and more importantly what bad things we may be doing.

In the last three decades a number of worldwide discussions and forums for policy making have underscored the responsibility of technology for sustainable development. For this paper, it is accepted that the traditional concept of sustainability by World Commission on Environment and Development (1987 UN) which defined sustainable development as 'development that meets the needs of the present without compromising the ability of future generations to meet their own needs'. In the context of technology and engineering it means that any engineering product must not serve the purpose of the present generation only (or more correctly, the owner of the company) but also consider its impact on the customers of present and future. As part of the US Centre for Sustainable Engineering study, Allen *et al.*, (2008) at the University of Texas at Austin, Carnegie Mellon University and Arizona State University have conducted a comprehensive review of accredited engineering programmes that incorporate sustainability concepts across the USA. Findings revealed alarmingly low participation (only 20% participated), but some disjoint efforts to inculcate sustainability in their syllabus, indicating some awareness about the urgent need. The authors stated forcefully: 'We believe a long-term goal of 21st century engineering education is to enable practicing engineers to incorporate tenets of sustainability into all phases of their practice, so that 'sustainable engineering' eventually equates with 'good engineering'."

Despite numerous discussion forums, the issue of sustainability still remains an elusive concept. In this chapter, the author intend to submit that while sustainability has occasionally been defined as anchored to social context, some of the psychosocial factors in evaluating sustainability, and particularly necessary in translating awareness about sustainability in pedagogy might be missing from most of the conceptualizations of the issue at hand. Most of the considerations about sustainability remain attached to physico-chemical impact only, if at all. The following are some of the statements that highlight the need for social sensitivity:

In 2009, the UK Engineering Council concluded in their report Guidance on Sustainability for the Engineering Profession: 'A purely environmental approach is insufficient, and increasingly engineers are required to take a wider perspective including goals such as poverty alleviation, social justice and local and global connections. The leadership and influencing role of engineers in achieving sustainability should not be under-estimated. Increasingly this will be as part of multi-disciplinary teams that include non-engineers, and through work that crosses national boundaries.' (ECUK, 2009).

However, sustainability, in practice, is mostly associated with eco-sensitivity of a physico-chemical nature. The terms society and culture are often used in the conference recommendations and criteria to be handed out, but their true meanings and application in appropriate context are sadly missing. The reason for this is probably the segregation of pedagogy and practice in science and technology, particularly in the engineering courses.

While we are slowly proceeding toward acknowledging the necessity of incorporating sustainability in the budding engineers, there are a few lacunae that the author would like to submit here. The author submits that technology has its profound impact on social environment as well, and society is not simply concerned with physico-chemical changes, but also with psychosocial changes that come with the rampant and greedy use of technology. Any endeavour to implement pedagogical changes without taking into account this psychological impact of technology is bound to be futile, as it cannot touch the ultimate seat of learning—the human mind. *To put it plainly, the pedagogy for technology and science, if needed to be made sensitive to human wellness, requires a deeper understanding of interrelation between man and nature, man and man, body and mind. In other words, we need a philosophy of technology.*

As a poignant example of psychological change as a result of technological intervention, we may take up the case of information technology. Information technology, characterized by high speed and an almost unlimited scope of variability is a great tool, which may be used for boon or bane. It is referred here particularly to the changing nature of human cognition and relationship by introducing an 'e-society' hitherto unknown. Information technology uses the power of symbolic communication to its ultimate extent. The evolution of man as a speaking animal changed the nature of relationship of the living world. As we assume that human beings are prone to read emotion in words and gestures/ facial-tonal expression in combination, how does the information age impact our relationships, when the earlier modicum of word-gesture combination is being manipulated in different ways through technological innovations?

Let us take the example of lying and deceiving. Indeed, the veridicality of communication is an important concern of human relationship. Before we could speak, there was little deception and violation of trust, as body postures used for communication is harder to be utilized for lying and deception. Ability to talk made us more versatile and more violating of other's rights. We can express love with and without loving; we can modulate others' emotion by words alone and by using the symbolic meaning of words with artistry. Of course, deception is one singular achievement of mankind. Only human beings can simulate a non-existing emotion, even through gestures without words (as in *Charlie Chaplin*). Probably it is only human beings who have the power to lie. Expressing emotion without concomitant physiological changes (that is through acting) is possible only for mankind. With this diabolical power in hand, the value judgment becomes the major safeguard against deception and demolition of civilization through intentional *misinformation*.

The entire issue of truth and deception has evolved as evolution has favoured words over gestures. The invention of telephone has opted out facial expressions, yet retaining the tonal quality of conversation. The e-society (the social network sites, the chat rooms) has done away with all non-verbal cues, and reading meaning into communication is reaching a new dimension. What characteristics do interpersonal sensitivity, responsibility and morality assume under these new technologically powerful medium of communication?

The knowledge of psychosocial responses to different uses of technology assumes more importance as application of scientific discoveries and engineering outputs pervade social domains. It is much easier to understand how the smoke emitting of a chimney affects the lungs of the inhabitants nearby. It is more difficult for the designing engineer to understand what emotional message the chimney gives to the inhabitants of a small village in the forest regarding the psychosocial changes. When projects of social engineering (for example, systematic training for ethnic handicrafts) are being brought to existence, the economic upgradation runs hand in hand with changes in social role and expectation. With each innovation we are unknowingly changing the existing platform of communication and relationship. Although this aspect has intrigued the literary pen from the very beginning, pedagogy has taken little attention to it.

We find that certain application of technology, even with a very positive intention often conveys opposite or confounding messages. We may see examples even outside information technology domain. I recall seeing a piece of designer jewellery eloquently announcing the company's love for nature by simulating a dead butterfly as ornament. Notwithstanding the originality and skill involved in the design, the message may be interpreted as acceptance of demolition of nature for self-adornment. Did the designer deliberately forward contradictory messages, or it was simple insensitivity? Can we sensitize our designer students toward the possible wrong message that may be conveyed and to the probable indicators of misapprehension? Can we inculcate a value system where the innovativeness may not overshadow the consideration for a good life?

In the age of information technology, a second psychological risk is the change in the cognitive system itself. The author is referring specifically to reallocation of attentional-resources. Many of the earlier notions of attention and memory are now being challenged in the face of unlimited flow of information. Here is an example. As we are getting more and more dependent on audio-visual medium of information, tools like animation and flickers are added to make the message more attractive. Now, as we know, the allocation of attentional-resources is determined by a number of external and internal factors. Traditionally physical characteristics like intensity, brightness, novelty, movement size etc. are known as external (objective) factors and interest, motivation and so on are known as internal (subjective) factors. In real life application, a balance of these two categories of factors finally decides the attentional resource allocation. The emphasis on innovativeness in information dissemination, often to produce quick and efficient results emphasize more on the external factors—and when they target the internal factors, they often do it by forcibly distorting some of the ingrained value systems, because after all if everybody is producing something novel, novelty is bound to be stereotyped.

We traditionally assume that after we are exposed to a new stimulus, we need some time to consolidate it, to associate with pre-existing memory elements and integrate them to produce a whole. When time is money, and plenty of information is needed to be disseminated within a very short time span, emphasis is on working upon immediate memory and on the basis of short term pleasure, rather than on assimilated ideas. Distractibility is bound to increase as a result of exposure to constant flow of diverse and often unrelated information. In other words, over-stimulation may take its toll on the individual.

It is in this context, the author submits the term *non-violation* in addition to the more familiar term 'sustainability'. The association of non-violation with non-violence is not perfunctory. Politically speaking, non-violence is a movement that is supposed to serve a power or weapon function against mainstream political tyranny. Non-violation is also a power against the mainstream (ab)use of science and technology, through a clear recognition of politicization of science as a deterrent to sustainable development. If systemic or holistic pedagogy needs to be seriously implemented, an explicit understanding that development needs to be open and proactively humane must be adopted. We need to consider not only the lungs and eyes and muscles of the stakeholders, but also protect the emotional dignity. If science is about truth, it should communicate clearly the incompleteness of truth. If technology is for development, it must communicate clearly those areas that cannot be taken care of. The stakeholders' dignity as a human being must not be molested. We cannot leave this judgment on the individual personality of the engineers. The curriculum needs to make a provision for this training. In other words, it is high time we modify our modules by deliberately introducing stimulation for thought processes that lead to physically and socially sustainable innovations. *That way, pedagogy becomes (or perhaps always was) part information and part activism.*

So, how far these may be reflected in pedagogical paradigm shift and actual classroom teaching of science and technology in India remains a matter to be scrutinized. Remembering Thomas Kuhn's notion of paradigm shift in his 'Structure of scientific revolutions' (1970), a creative change may be incorporated to introduce systemic learning programmes to facilitate students' sensitivity to sustainable engineering innovations. If we recapitulate Kuhn's seminal work we may recall that he designated 'normal science' as one that assumes truth to be known clearly, and that paradigm shifts occur when an anomaly in the given paradigm is detected. The traditional paradigm of engineering education is now in ardent need of shift.

For example, Salama (2005) argues that for architectural pedagogy, to be humane, it needs the following shifts in paradigm:

- Things versus Relations between Things
- Economy and Ecology: Isolation versus Integration
- Fight versus Fit with Nature: Techno-development versus Eco-development
- Mechanistic Pedagogy versus Systemic Pedagogy

All these are easier said than done. We need to be truly mindful about revising our pedagogy to make this shift. As educationists, we cannot control the pressure of the investing companies on the engineers. But we can mould the mind of the budding engineers to be a moral contributor as well as a technological one.

Laws pertaining to the preservation of environment and impact on human health need to be emphasized in the curriculum, as very few of us know precisely our own and others' legal rights and responsibilities regarding environmental preservation. Knowing and critiquing the law of the land is not enough. Actual change may be brought about if and only if the motivation for sustainable and eco-friendly innovation is promoted in the student community. Here the role of value education comes to achieve a position of prominence.

If we agree that morality and value judgments need to be part and parcel of teaching science and technology, what should be the highlights? In all engineering curriculum, there are sideline courses of literature and social sciences, presumably with the idea that knowing science is not all. But these subjects are underdogs and often are designed by experts of mainstream literature and social science subjects and the curriculum often reflects a précis of the original syllabus as a whole. There are very few curricula that actually relate the different subjects. In any case, with the heavy schedule of engineering curriculum, it is actually difficult for the students to attend to and integrate the subsidiary subjects, and these papers remain more of entertainment and relaxation between 'heavy' classes. Given that technology students of good institutions are often the best ones in the country, it is likely that at least some of them will be responsible not only for designing instruments and commodities but also for designing policy. Therefore, sustainability and non-violation of others' rights need to be an integral part of their thought process as well which can rarely be driven home through theoretical discussion only.

The argument to be made in this context is that this change requires re-viewing the essences of teaching learning processes in pedagogy. The role of individualized learning needs to be adjudicated in this context. While traditional Gurukul process of our country catered to individualized learning, the thrust on mass learning customs and batch processes, where equal amount of learning for all individuals is the stated objective, has been the call of the day for the last few centuries. Individualized active learning has been proposed for quite some time in the context of sustainable development training for science and technology students. Since non-violation and concern for sustainability is an intrinsic value system, it would never be embedded in human heart by rhetorical information alone. It needs a curriculum that involves hand-on-job; stimulating thinking that involves designing with a social awareness and rewarding socially relevant thinking.

One such experiment had been done in MIT at the turn of this century, where an experiment known as 'ThinkCycle' was conducted. This was a student based programme of designing where assignments were given to the students for designing with global collaboration and social awareness. The students also used the advantage of open source (GNU) in computer, which is, by itself, an active step in non-violation of the dignity of human knowledge. The work was initiated in consultation with the Media Lab Professor Mitchell Resnick, and a pilot design studio course was named 'Design those matters'. The studio course aimed at the students being able to take up real life challenges posited by the NGOs to cater to underserved communities. Gradually many other Universities and organizations participated, including Harvard. Thus from the very inception it was a socially responsible project. Specifically, the students had to think of designs which would be sustainable in all senses, directed toward human good and protective from evil outcome. At each step, the students released the design in open forum, received critiques and suggestions and the final outcome was a collaborative innovation.

When the programme was evaluated, a number of interesting elements came up. Some of the positive feedbacks on the part of the students were: Exposure to real world problem, opportunity to learn by doing, being socially relevant and enjoying collaboration. However, the resistances to collaboration were also important. Some major causes of resistance were the feeling of being competitive, although few attributed it to the project itself, but considered it to be more due to the nature of use of designs in organizations. Other barriers were the feeling of exposing premature ideas, being too taxing on themselves as they had to expose things before thinking it to its fullest extent, and about 12 per cent considered that others would benefit from it without benefiting themselves. Thus competitiveness ingrained in external and internal factors were the major barriers.

These resistances are likely to come up with even greater emphasis when such programmes would be launched in real life technology application. I submit that the resistances reflect a conflict of value between individualism and collectivism. We know that the American industries are more prone to promote individual achievement, while countries like Japan, advanced in technological sense as much as US, still focuses on a collective contribution. Even without going deep into East-west dichotomy, we may recall that there is an inherent contradiction in western pedagogy, where equal opportunity of learning for all is eulogized *vis-à-vis* individual achievement and competitiveness. Everybody must have motivation to reach the top, which, often perversely promotes unhealthy competition and ruthlessness. This inherent competitiveness with a semblance of democracy is definitely deceitful and psychologically harmful to say the least.

Recently Information and communication technology (ICT) is being recommended as an approach for individualized teaching-learning tool. This new technology may be used or abused for bringing about immense change in society—for or against sustainability. Either way, ICT is going to assume significant role in teaching-learning in near future. Systematic research needs to be carefully designed to examine how the basic cognitive processes, whose use has been apparently well understood in traditional teaching learning process, may acquire new meaning and relevance in the context of ICT based pedagogy. Specifically, ICT may be used to provide scope for practicing eco-sensitivity and social awareness as an integral part of project designs and the reward may be so adjusted that efficiency becomes synonymous with non-violation. Contrarily, the same technique may be used to promote self-centered and individualized competition, to enhance the mutual segregation among learners.

In the future pedagogy, as individualized models of e-education are bound to come up, we need to remember the significance of collaborative real life training, and the sense of responsibility needs to be imbibed in the students. The responsibility must not only be about delivering the product in time with maximum efficiency, but also on sensitivity about its psychosocial and physical impact. The studio approach of learning, hitherto not explored well in our country needs to be incorporated as there have been studies indicating that this approach inculcates greater flexibility and originality in thinking as compared to directed and closely supervised teaching (Lynch, Goold and Blain, 2004).

However, one interesting finding of Lynch et al.'s study was that when the student's preferences for directional, traditional and studio approaches were assessed, it was found that students preferred clearly defined variables and close supervision. Its implication is that if we train our students to be lazy, they will remain lazy. Therefore, probably we need to begin at the beginning by inculcating critical thinking in the students. Suggestions of critical pedagogy have come from some Marxist educationists. For example, Moraes (2003) reports an interview with Peter McLaren, where he suggests that challenging the existing semiotics of pedagogy is a sine qua non of critical education.

Why is critical thinking development essential for technology students? It is required because many projects pay a lip service to sustainability. The very word 'development' looks to the future and promises good to the future generation. The students of technology need to be aware that not all such promises are carried out in the designs that are produced. Practice from student life to work with collective intelligence would enable them to find out the loopholes and proceed for a truly sustainable design.

In a special lecture on 'Major challenges in integrating sustainable development in Technical and Vocational Education & Training (TVET), at the International experts meeting on reorienting TVET policy towards education for sustainable development, Berlin, Germany, Dr. S. Majumdar (2009) highlighted the social and economic context of sustainability as an integral part of Education of sustainable development (ESD). He identified a number of challenges:

Challenge 1: Understanding the Meaning and Scope of ESD

Challenge 2: Defining Sustainable Development Skills in terms of KSA (Knowledge, Skill, and Attitude)

Challenge 3: Applying functional models for integrating SD in TVET Curriculum

Challenge 4: Relating Generic to Specific Learning Outcomes in SD

Challenge 5: Integrating Sustainable Development in Subject Domain

Challenge 6: Imparting ESD with innovative pedagogy

While each of these challenges require detailed understanding, I submit in this context that the final solution to each of these challenges would include a different kind of integrational capacity not reflected in good academic results only, nor in high marks in mathematics, chemistry and physics. The attitudinal and emotional issues, the selective orientation of memory toward human communication and emotion, empathic understanding of the impact of a particular design are needed to truly create an atmosphere for sustainability and non-violation of dignity. Thus a reorientation of the learning skills is required.

In the present chapter it is argued that innovative technical designing with eco-sensitivity in mind requires a re-allocation of memory, attention, problem solving modes and decision making, not hereto tapped in traditional teaching-learning process. The role of selective memory, easy shift between suspended and focussed attention, relative immunity from distraction in an age of speed, yet keeping up the speed itself, the prioritization of issues, profitable yet non-violating decision making etc. may require a different kind of skill, or perhaps a different and flexible use of executive functions of the brain. Such skills have been used intuitively by a handful of creative persons, but not explored and understood enough to be put to use for changing the spirit of the curricula. This lacuna takes us directly into the issue of how to develop this special kind of competency. It is high time we find practical ways to develop not only individualized intelligence and competency, but also collective competency and an ingrained sensitivity to the social value of innovation. Creativity is not all about originality and effectiveness. It is also about sensitivity. We do not know yet, in terms of brain mechanisms, how morality and cognitive skills operate in conjunction for creativity. Down-to-earth plans need to be forwarded for research in cognitive exploration to help modify the pedagogic challenges in science and technical education.

Last but not the least, the author asserts that in this chapter she has used the terms science and technology together. It is not only because the boundary between the two is softening in the last few decades. Indeed, she consider these two as different. But sensitivity for sustainability and non-violation is associated not only with technology but also with pure science, because the ethereal existence of pure science suddenly becomes malicious technology even without the full understanding of the pure scientist. The nuclear bomb in relation to Einstein is just a well known example. If we recall the age old yet ever fresh taxonomy of Bloom, pure science is more of cognition, while technology is an amalgam of cognition and psychomotor properties. The affective element is missing as being 'non-science'. We need to remember that emotion may be our major building block for inculcating eco-sensitivity and non-violation in transformative pedagogy.

REFERENCES

Ali, N. (2007). *Engineering Interventions for Higher and Sustainable Agricultural Growth in India.* Paper presented at the TC meeting of APCAEM, 20-21 Nov., Bejing.

Allen, D., Allenby, B., Bridges, M., Crittenden, J., Davidson, C., Hendrickson, C., Matthews, C., Murphy, C. and Pijawka, D., (2008). *Benchmarking Sustainability Engineering Education: Final Report,* Pittsburgh, PA, USA: Centre for Sustainable Engineering. Url: http://www.csengin.org/benchmark.htm

Byrne, E., Desha, C., Fitzpatrick, J. and Hargroves, K. (2010). *Engineering Education for Sustainable Development: A Review of International Progress.* 3rd International Symposium for Engineering Education, 2010, University College Cork, Ireland. http://www.thinkcycle.org/dtm

Lynch, K., Goold, A., and Blain, J. (2004). Students' pedagogical preferences in the delivery of IT capstone courses. *Issues in Informing Science and Information Technology,* 1, 431-442.

Martin, B. (1999). Ttechnology, Violence, and Peace in *Encyclopedia of Violence, Peace, and Conflict,* Volume 3 (Lester R. Kurtz, Editor-in-Chief) (New York: Academic Press,), pp. 447-459.

Massaquoi, J.G.M. (2009). Strengthening Peace Building through Science and Technology Education. *Science Education International.* 20, 1/2, 5-24.

Moraes, M. (2003). The Path of Dissent: An Interview with Peter McLaren. *Journal of Transformative Education* 2003 1: 117-134. http://jtd.sagepub.com/content/1/2/117

Prestero, T.J., Height, M.J., Hwang, R. 2001. Rapid Cholera Treatment: Exploring Alternative IV Treatment Devices. *Development by Design, Workshop on Collaborative Open Source Design of Appropriate Technologies,* MIT, Cambridge. http://www.thinkcycle.org/tc-papers/?paper_id=12060

Salama, A. (2005). *Skill-based/Knowledge-Based Architectural Pedagogies: An Argument for Creating Humane Environments.* 7th Intl Conference on Humane Habiate-ICHH-05 – The International Association of Humane Habitat IAHH. Rizvi College of Architecture, Mumbai, India. January 29-31.

3

The Changing Face of Human Resource Management in Education for the Sustainable Development in the Era of Globalisation

Yazali Josephine

Globalization is characterized by increasing worldwide competition and accelerating economic change that brings unpredictable outcomes to ensure India's competitiveness, which both the public and private sectors have taken steps to be knowledge intensive and knowledge enable with emphasis on its human resource development strategy. To unleash the full potential of its human capital in the public sector the human resource management initiatives, that have been formulated and implemented include review of its remuneration system, enhancement of its training and development activities particularly in management development, and in the use of information and communication technology in the public service for the sustainable development.

Globalization: Changes and Challenges for Education in India

The principal objective of education has been the development every individual, the minimum level of education that is essential to achieve this goal in the agrarian society. In the present borderless information society, education needs to be able to respond to additional demands of a rapidly globalizing world by raising awareness of environment, peace, cultural and social diversity, increased competitiveness, and the concept of a global village. Such education is to a knowledge or information society what secondary education was to an industrial economy. Education prepares the individual to connect and live in harmony with the environment around him. Globalization has changed the size, nature and quality of that environment. The challenge for higher education, therefore, is to reform, create and develop systems that prepare the individual to work in a borderless economy and live in a global society. In other words, our educational institutions need to produce global citizens.

With the globalization gaining momentum, market substituted political ideology as the dominant force guiding national and global policies. What followed next, therefore, does not seem so illogical. National governments everywhere, partly in deference to the ascendancy of the market and partly in response to pressure from the private sector to expand their sphere of activities, began to relinquish control over the delivery of social goods. Everything began to be viewed as a commodity that could be produced and delivered by the private sector in line with market forces and according to the principles of supply and demand. One by one—water, electricity, postal services, health, and now education, have been turned into a commodity.

The withdrawal of state from higher education has also been helped by economists, who have had an overly simple way of assessing the return on investments in higher education. The basic problem is that they have measured the return on education exclusively through wage differentials. With reference to someone who has no education, someone who has been to primary school, someone who has completed secondary school, and someone with a university degree, one can ask how much more each earns than the previous. These differences are then compared to the incremental amounts invested in their education to find the return. The results generally suggest that higher education yields a lower return than primary or secondary education—and they have been used to justify the skewing of government budgets and development funds away from higher education institutions.

The rate of return calculations are flawed because they do not take account of the full range of benefits to those who receive higher education. For example, higher education can enhance health, openness, peace, and social development, and at the same time reduce disease, bigotry and blind nationalism—so the private benefits to the individual and to society are not just the direct labour productivity benefits, as the rate of return analysis suggests.

Higher education confers benefits above and beyond enhancing the incomes of those who receive it. And many of these benefits take the form of public goods, such as the contribution of higher education to enterprise, leadership, governance, culture, and participatory democracy, and its potential for lifting the disadvantaged out of poverty. These are all vital building blocks for stronger economies and societies and all routes by which the benefit of investment in higher education multiplies throughout society.

Liberal democracies have traditionally operated on the principle of separation of activities in the social sphere just as they have on the principle of separation of powers in the political sphere. The private sector had been given a relatively free hand in the production and delivery of economic goods while the state concentrated on the provision of healthcare, education and other infrastructure goods, also known as public goods. Globalization has changed all that. The rapid expansion of the influence of the private sector at the global level necessitated a corresponding expansion in their sphere of activities by diversifying into the production and delivery of public goods that had always been within the purview of the state. The takeover was swift and remarkable in the sense that the effort did not meet much resistance.

One of the major consequences of the globalization of education has been commodification and the corporatization of institutions of higher learning. It is said that the for-profit education market in the United States is worth more than $500 billion in revenue for the involved corporates. More than one thousand state schools have been handed over to corporations to be run as businesses. But there is a fundamental problem with the way business models have been applied to the delivery of education and other public goods. Unthinking adoption of the private sector model prevents the development of a meaningful approach to management in the public services in general or to the social services in particular based on their distinctive purposes, conditions and objectives.

There is another, more serious, problem with corporatization of education. Corporations operate on the principles of cost reduction and profit maximization. These require introducing standardization and the packaging of product in compact, measurable, byte-like, configuration. Applied to education, these approaches would possibly negate its basic fabric and purpose. Education has always encouraged and represents openness, inquiry, diversity, research and limitless learning. Corporatization of education would make it elitist—the one provided by corporations for the masses and the poor who cannot afford going to the traditional institutions of learning, and the other for the rich and the affluent.

The delivery of public goods and services is and should remain the primary responsibility of the state. Representative government may not be the ideal or perfect arrangement for governance but it represents the best that is available, and certainly more desirable than the private sector management of public services such as education. If the state relinquishes its control over education and education policy, we run the risk of diminishing it to the status of a packaged for-profit product which it is not. Openness, diversity, scholarship, research and disinterested learning will be its biggest victims.

Sustainable Development: Urgent Need

Economic development is closely associated with poverty reduction in many countries. It is also believed that increased income levels lead to improved health, education and living standards. However, development experiences show that there is no automatic link between increased per capita income and reduction in poverty levels. Absolute poverty is a condition of life characterized by malnutrition, illiteracy and diseases beneath any reasonable definition of human decency. Poverty not only reflects an impoverished state in which people live but also a lack of opportunity to choose other types of living and lack of capacity to choose even when opportunities are available. Poverty is ultimately a matter of capability deprivation (Amartya Sen, 1990).

In India, reduction of poverty has been one of the major concerns of development planning. The elimination of substantial famines in the post-independence period is a reflection of successful efforts to reduce poverty. Poverty in India is measured in terms of 'poverty line' which is based on an absolute minimum level of per capita consumption. In the 60s, the poverty line was estimated on the basis of expenditure required for minimum food intake: 2,400 calories in rural areas and 2,100 calories in the urban areas. Based on this norm, it was estimated that ₹ 20 per person in rural areas and ₹ 25 per person in urban areas are the least necessary monthly incomes to partake the basic calorie requirements.

Indian planners, it seems, believed in the initial stages that economic growth will have a trickle-down effect on poverty. However, it was soon recognised that poverty reduction may not be possible in the near future if we rely only on a top-down approach. Hence, programmes directly addressing the issue of poverty were envisaged as part of the planning process itself. The anti-poverty programmes that gained momentum in the 70s are a reflection of this changing strategy. The integrated rural development programmes aimed at the creation of assets and employment in rural areas. The National Rural Employment Programme (NREP) and Rural Labour Employment Guarantee Programme (RLEGP) are two such examples of anti-poverty initiatives. All such efforts were to reduce poverty through income-generating strategies. In other words, poverty reduction is seen essentially as a process of enhancing income levels of the poor. This means it is not a sustainable method to eradicate poverty.

Development now is defined in terms of human development. 'Human Development is the end—economic growth is the means' (UNDP 1996). Literacy and education have a direct role in human development and are instrumental in facilitating other achievements. Investments in the social sector in developing countries lead to higher literacy rates and higher enrolment rates. For example, between 1970 and 1993 literacy rates in less developed countries increased by half, from 43 per cent to 61 per cent. South Asia has the lowest level (49%) of literacy as against Latin America where the literacy rate is 86 per cent. Similarly, between 1961 and 1991 Net Enrolment Ratios (NET) in developing countries increased from 48 per cent to 77 per cent (UNDP 1996).

It is now universally recognised that literacy and education enhance human capabilities. Hence, efforts to reduce and ultimately eliminate illiteracy lead to human development in the short run and poverty reduction in the long run. However, India's record on this count is far from satisfactory. India's success in removing poverty, ignorance, disease and inequality of opportunities has been even markedly less substantial than that of many other countries. And in one particular field—elementary education—India stands considerably behind the average of the poorest countries in the world (Dreze and Sen 1995: 3). Various ways of making the economy sustainable can be introduced in the school or literacy curriculum. The teaching-learning method is a vital way to sensitise people to this issue.

At present provision of education and health facilities are seen as part of some anti-poverty programmes in India. While the long term contribution of education to poverty reduction is accepted, direct intervention in education as part of anti-poverty programmes is less emphasized. Investments in education in the recent past have, however, increasingly targeted primary education and adult literacy programmes that benefit the poor. The flows of external funds to primary education in the 90s have also contributed to an increase in total investment in primary education.

The relationship between education and sustainable development is complex. In general research shows that basic education is key to a nation's ability to develop and achieve sustainability targets. Research has shown that education can improve agriculture productivity, enhance the status of women, reduce population growth rates, enhance environmental protection, and generally raise the standard of living. But the relationship is not linear. For example, four to six years of education is the minimum threshold for increasing agricultural productivity. Literacy and numeration allow farmers to adopt new agricultural methods, take risks and respond to market signals. A basic education also helps farmers gain title to their land and apply for credit at banks and other lending institutions. Moreover, education benefits women in life-altering ways. Education thus directly affects sustainability plans in three ways: implementation, decision making and improving the quality of life.

Sustainable human development is people-centered and implies that patterns of development should be sustained in the future as well; what is does not envisage is the perpetuation of existing inequities in the future. The essence of sustainable development is that everyone should have equal access to development opportunities in the present and in future (UNDP 1994). Therefore investments in education should be perceived from this angle. There is a need to closely scrutinise project approaches and activities that have directly linked poverty reduction with sustainable development.

Education for Sustainable Development

Education for Sustainable Development (ESD) is a vision of education that seeks to empower people to assume responsibility for creating a sustainable future. Central to ESD is the concept of culture as an essential underlying theme. It has been acknowledged that there is no "single route" to sustainable development. Further, it is clear that understandings of, and visions for, sustainability will be different for each of us and that we will need to work together to negotiate the process of achieving sustainability. There are many different stakeholders in sustainable development (i.e., governments, businesses, educational institutions, media, youth, etc). Each of these sectors has a different vision of sustainable development and how it can contribute. Some are interested in environmental preservation and protection, some have economic development interests while others may be more interested in social development. In addition, how each nation, cultural group and individual views sustainable development will depend on its own values. The values held in a society help define how personal decisions are made and how national legislation is written (UNESCO (2005).

The challenge is to bring these different stakeholders together so that they may collaborate in partnerships to find a balance between their interests and priorities. Various approaches to ESD encourage people to understand the complexities of, and synergies between, the issues threatening planetary sustainability and understand and assess their own values and those of the society in which they live in the context of sustainability.

Globalization and Human Resource Management in India: Change Adopted for Sustainable Development

The economic reforms announced by the Government change the direction of the country from socialistic pattern to market economy. The trends of market economy result in intense and vibrant competition, entry of new multinationals and consolidation of existing multinationals increasing the stake of multinationals in their Indian partnerships, intensification of competition due to import liberalization, increased competition due to the emergence of buyer's market and changed notions about small scale industry. The vulnerability of Indian Industry and frequent changes in international environment are other basic causes for competition. Thus, the major result of economic reforms is competition and all-round competition. This situation necessitated for the Total quality and Productivity Management (TQPM) and minimization of cost through attracting positive factors and eliminating hindering factors.

Now, the survival and development of industry in India, mostly depends on its ability to compete with other Indian firms, multinationals and in foreign markets. The ability to maintain high quality and maximize productivity determine the competitive ability of Indians firms, which in turn is largely dependent on the quality and commitment of human resources.

The Strategy in India: Education and HR Development

Knowledge is the driving force in the rapidly changing globalised economy and society. Quantity and quality of specialized human resources determine their competence in the global market. Emergence of knowledge as driving factor results in both challenges and opportunities. It is well known that the growth of the global economy has increased opportunities for those countries with good levels of education.

Globalization has a multi-dimensional impact on the system of education. It promotes new tools and techniques in this area like

E-learning, Flexible learning, Distance Education Programmes and Overseas training. Globalization will mean many different things for education. In the near future, "it will mean a more competitive and deregulated educational system modeled after free market but with more pressure on it to assure that the next generation of workers are prepared for some amorphous 'job market of 21st century'.

Since "Life long jobs have been converted in to yearly contracts there is still possibility of even short duration jobs. Our education system should deliver such education and training so that professionals can adjust themselves as per market expectations. Globalisation has underlined the need for reforms in the educational system with particular reference to the wider utilization of information technology, giving productivity dimension to education and emphasis on its research and development activities.

India is also following the global phenomenon. As part of globalization, the economic reform packages were introduced in India in the beginning of 1991. These reform packages imposed a heavy compression on the public budgets on education sector, more specifically so on higher education. This has trickled down to public expenditure on education in general, and higher education in particular.

Indian government and Indian corporate sector has recognized the importance of management education in the changing global scenario. Today under the reforming economic conditions, integration of the Indian economy with world economy presupposes efficiency and competitiveness in the domestic front as well as in the international arena. As the process of globalization is technology-driven, and knowledge-driven, the very success of economic reform policies critically depends upon the competence of human capital.

But, what is observed is the reverse. Even within the education sector, relative priority assigned to higher education has been on the decline. It is to be realized that higher education institutions play an important role in setting the academic standard for primary and secondary education. They are also responsible for not only providing the specialized human capital in order to corner the gains from globalization, but also for training inside the country, provide policy advice, etc.

Globalization is expected to have a positive influence on the volume, quality and spread of knowledge through increased interaction among the various states.

Today our educational system is strong enough but Central and state governments should change their roles within the education system, reinventing themselves as facilitating and supervisory organizations. Teacher training, infrastructure and syllabuses need to be urgently upgraded. Industry should come forward to share experience with students and to offer more opportunities for live Projects.

The free market philosophy has already entered the educational world in a big way. Commercialization of education is the order of the day. Commercial institutions offering specialized education have come up everywhere. In view of globalization, many corporate universities, both foreign and Indian, are encroaching upon our government institutions.

Our Institutes like IIMs and IITs have produced world class professionals. These institutes impart quality education as per industry expectations and give due importance to Institute Industry Interface. Under the new scenario, Government—Private partnership is becoming important in Management Education. Now India is a transforming country. We are near to achieve status of developed nation.

The demand for higher education has been growing rapidly with comparatively faster growth in enrolment in higher educational institutions than the growth in number of higher educational institutions. The growth rates are doubled among the students enrolled in post-graduate and research, while the number of institutions for post-graduate and research studies has grown at a slower rate in 1990s than in 1980s.

Though the enrolment has been increasing in absolute terms, only 7 per cent of the population in the age group 17 to 24 attended higher educational institutions in India, as against 92 per cent of the eligible age-group population attending higher educational institutions in USA, 52 per cent in UK and 45 per cent in Japan.

In India, over the years, there have been private initiatives in education initially for philanthropic reasons and eventually in professional and even in general higher education not only to meet the growing demands but also to realize the huge and quick profits potential. This was situational because government has shortage of funds so for the benefit of nation government allowed private institutions.

Privatization of higher education has emerged in several forms and types in the recent decade in India. One, privatization within government higher education institutions takes place in the form of introducing self-financing courses within government institutions; two, converting government-aided private institutions into private self financing institutions; three, allowing to expand self-financing private institutions with recognition and also without recognition, which may be termed as commercial private. Commercial private higher education emerges from market forces and tied to economic and global forces.

They thrive on the principles of commercialism, primarily focus on vocational courses and are highly pragmatic. Their commercial thrust is training jobs; indeed, part of the curriculum is industrial training. Not only training for jobs but also place their students in well-paid jobs. This indeed speaks about the strong industry—institution linkages. They are narrowly focused, rather micro-specific in designing their course and training. This narrow focus is their strength as well weakness. It is strength as long as there is demand for such specific nature of the courses and a weakness once such a demand is satiated. Moreover, the built-in set up/ infrastructure do not allow them to diversify. They cater to the unmet demands or rather demand- absorbing from the non-university higher education sector.

We can divide these institutions in to various types, like of the self-financing engineering colleges and management institutions are affiliated to the conventional universities In which, the course structure, design, curriculum, and the pattern of examination fall withinthe purview of the national or state pattern. On the other side, several of these self-financing private institutions are also non-affiliating to any universities and cater to the demands of the corporate sector nationally and internationally.

This privatization has its negative impact also. Student act as the market force. Students have the power while faculty is weak in these private institutions. Indeed, the faculty lacks the position, power and autonomy as they traditionally enjoyed at universities. Basically they serve to students and their practical orientations in commercial private institutions. These institutions rely on part-time faculty and may be drawn from full-time faculty at public universities (and hence do not add to further employment opportunities). When employing full-time faculty, they pay meager salary. Perhaps many of them have neither practical nor academic expertise and lack training.

Globalization leads to challenges and threats also. The major concern is to deliver world-class education with updated curriculum and practical exposure. This is possible only by attracting talented and experienced persons in to academics.

At present it is difficult to assess not only the nature and dimensions of globalization, but also what it means to the field of education. A few educational researchers have attempted to make connections between the several dimensions of globalization and the policies of education.

India is witnessing new era in the field of Management Education. Many Corporate groups like Reliance, Nirma, Tata, Sterlite etc., are promoting Management Institutes. Some reputed foreign universities are also coming to India. But Government should issue some guidelines so that fees structure remains within certain limit and those who are from economically poor background have same opportunities in accessing education at such Institutes.

Strategic Educational Planning for Human Capital Formation: Why Change in Educational Planning is Essential?

The benefits of globalization accrue to the countries with highly skilled human capital and it is a curse for the countries without such specialized human capital. Developing and transition countries are further challenged in a highly competitive world economy because their higher education systems are not adequately developed for the creation and use of knowledge. Converting the challenges into opportunities depend on the rapidity at which they adapt to the changing environment.

One of the noteworthy features of the Indian workplace is demographic uniqueness. It is estimated that both China and India will have a population of 1.45 billion people by the year 2030; however, India will have a larger workforce than China. Indeed, it is likely India will have 986 million people of working age in 2030, which will probably be about 300 million more than in 2007. And by 2050, it is expected India will have 230 million more workers than China and about 500 million more than the United States of America (U.S.). It may be noted that half of India's current population of 1.1 billion people are under of 25 years of age (Chatterjee 2006). While this fact is a demographic dividend for the economy, it is also a danger sign for the country's ability to create new jobs at an unprecedented rate.

When India's young demographic bubble begins to reach working age, India will need far more jobs than currently exist to keep living standards from declining. India today doesn't have enough good jobs for its existing workers, much less for millions of new ones. If it cannot better educate its children and create jobs for then once they reach working age, India faces a population time bomb: The nation will grow poorer and not richer, with hundred of millions of people stuck in poverty.

In Indian an emerging dominant perspective is the influence of globalization on technological advancements, business management, education and communication infrastructures is leading to a converging effect on managerial mindsets and business behaviours. And when India embraced liberalization and economic reform in the early 1990s, dramatic changes were set in motion in terms of corporate mindsets and Human

Resource Management practices as a result of global imperatives and accompanying changes in societal priorities. Indeed, the onset of a burgeoning competitive service sector compelled a demographic shift in worker educational status and heightened the demand for job relevant skills as well as regional diversity. Expectedly, there has been a marked shift towards valuing human resources (HR) in Indian organizations as they become increasingly strategy driven as opposed to the culture of the status quo.

With 21st century India burdened with the world's largest population of illiterate citizens, an estimated 59 million children in the six-14 age group out of school, and huge number of job-seekers across the country having swollen to 41 million—not because there aren't sufficient jobs, but because youth streaming out of the obsolete education system are unemployable—alarm sirens are wailing in all sections of Indian society. As the new millennium challenges are for the quality education, a strategic educational planning is the best social leveler and passport to gainful employment affluence and social respect. Hence despite the rig ours government permit system, there is a flurry of activity in terms of promotion of new schools, colleges and institutes of professional education. in higher education the bar is continuously being raised given the steadily rising demand for quality higher—especially professional—study programmes

Conclusion

Globalization is an extremely powerful ideology. It is repeatedly being total that there is no alternative to it. Even Amartya Sen has taken this position. There is a feeling of helplessness when globalization is represented as being the inevitable outcome of technological development. If globalization is here to stay then serious measures have to be adopted to bridge the divide, which could increase the inequalities like Inequalities among people, even inequalities among sectors of education etc.

The Dakar World Education Forum also recommended with particular to enhancing access and improving the relevance, effectiveness and equity in education which are very utmost important in this era of globalization. They also recommended that there should be a policy dialogue on education reforms. Particular emphasis was placed on selected key issues, notably those of equity in and access to secondary education (especially with regard to gender and marginalized groups), the renewal of content and teaching/learning processes (especially science/technology-related subjects), harmonizing youth programmes and policies with the provision of secondary education, and the promotion of life skills and counseling programmes. Other issues will include the role of teachers, the involvement of new education actors, school management and the learning environment. The use of art and cultural activities will also be promoted as effective approaches to facilitate the development of learners' creativity and critical thinking. Best practices should be drawn from a variety of social and cultural contexts and, disseminated and promoted, with a particular focus on alternative access routes into education, education for responsible behaviours, approaches to counseling adolescents, the participation of new education actors and partners, and the renewal of secondary education contents, methods and management (both at central and school levels). Policy dialogue and networking will be promoted through inter-agency collaboration and cooperation with NGOs; students' groups and parents' associations should work on Secondary Education Reforms. Advocacy efforts, strategic educational planning in building human capital should be undertaken to promote a new vision of education among decision-makers.

REFERENCES

AICTE (1994). Report of the High Power Committee for Mobilization of Additional Resources for Technical Education, All India Council for Technical Education, New Delhi.

Government of India (1997). Approach Paper to the Ninth Five Year Plan: 1997-2002, Planning Commission, New Delhi.

Reports of UGC, AICTE & Ministry of HRD-Government of India.

Armstrong, Michael (1999). *A Handbook of Human Resource Management Practice.* Kogan Page Limited.

Burstiner, Irving. *The Small Business Handbook.* Prentice Hall, 1988.

Dreze, J. and Sen, A. (eds.) (1998). *Indian Development. Selected Regional Perspectives.* Delhi: Oxford University Press.

Giddens, A. (1994). *Beyond Left and Right.* Polity Press: Cambridge.

Green, Paul C. (199). *Building Robust Competencies: Linking Human Resource Systems to Organizational Strategies.* Jossey-Bass.

Gubman, Edward L. (1996). "The Gauntlet is Down." *Journal of Business Strategy.* November-December.

Harris, J. (2001). Globalization and World's Poor Institutions, Inequality and Justice. *Economic and Political Weekly.* June 9-15, 2001, Vol. XXXVI No. 23

James, E. (1987). The public/Private Division of Responsibility for Education: An International Comparison. *Economics of Education Review.* Vol. 6(1), pp. 1-14.

Jawaharlal Nehru University and National Commission for Unorganised Enterprises.

Jha, U.S., and Pujari, P. (eds). (1996). *Indian Women Today. Tradition, Modernity and Challenge*. New Delhi: Kanishka Publishers.

Johnston, John. (1996). "Time to Rebuild Human Resources." *Business Quarterly.* Winter.

Josephine, Yazali. (2003). *Globalisation and Challenges for Education: Focus on Equity and Equality.* New Delhi: Shipra Publication.

Kelkar, V.L. and Rao, V.V.B. (1996). *India Development Policy Imperatives.* New Delhi: Tata McGraw Hill.

Landes, D. (1998). *The Wealth and Poverty of Nations: Why Some are So Rich and Some So Poor*. London: Little, Brown and Co.

Nair, R.G. and D. Ajit (1984). Parellel Colleges in Kerala: Enrollment, Costs and Employment, *Economic and Political Weekly*, 19(42&43) Oct. 20-27.

Rao, K.S. and Singh, M. (2002). Self-Financed Courses in Universities and Colleges. *University News*, Vol. 40 (43).

Ravi Srivastav paper on: Disparities in Access to Higher Education in India,

Reece, Barry L., and Rhonda Brandt (1993). *Effective Human Relations in Organizations.* Boston: Houghton Mifflin.

Roberts, Gary, Gary Seldon, and Carlotta Roberts. *Human Resources Management.* Washington, D.C.: Small Business Administration, n.a.

Rossiter, Jill A. (1996). *Human Resources: Mastering Your Small Business.* Upstart Publishing.

Sethi, R.M. (eds.) (1999). *Globalization, Culture and Women's Development.* New Delhi: Rawat Publications.

Solomon, Charlene Marmer. "Working Smarter: How HR Can Help." *Personnel Journal.* June 1993.

Tilak, J.B.G. (1991). The Privatisation of Higher Education. *Prospects*, Vol. XXL (2).

Tinker, I. (1990). Persistent Inequalities Women and World Development. New York: Oxford University Press.

UNDP (United Nations Development Programme) (1999). *Human Development Report*. New York: Oxford University Press.

UNDP (1997). *Human Development Report*. New York: Oxford University Press.

UNDP (2001). *Human Development Report*. New York: Oxford University Press.

Ulrich, Dave (1998). *Delivering Results: A New Mandate for HR Professionals.* Harvard Business School Press.

4

Education for Sustainable Development

An Approach Towards Future World

Sanat K. Ghosh

Education for Sustainable Development (ESD) is an emerging concept in the discipline of 'education' as a very significant multi-disciplinary area of study. The present chapter draws the basic conceptual frame of ESD from the Report of the World Commission on Environment and Development (1987). Sustainable development is not a fixed state of harmony, but rather a process of change in which the exploitation of resources, the direction of investments, the orientation of technological development, and institutional change are made consistent with future as well as present needs. ESD is a dynamic concept that utilizes all aspects of public awareness, education and training to create or enhance an understanding of the linkages among the issues of sustainable development. It has a vision to balance human and economic well-being with cultural traditions and respect for the earth's natural resources through trans-disciplinary educational methods and approaches and ethics for lifelong learning with a sense of global solidarity.

Background

The concept of sustainable development was popularized in 1987 with the publication of the 'Brundtland Report'—the Report of the World Commission on Environment and Development. This landmark report highlighted the need to conceptualize sustainable development that would "meet the needs of the present without compromising the ability of future generations to meet their own needs".

Until recently, the planet has been a large world in which human activities and their effects are tied to neatly compartmentalize within nations or within sectors, viz., energy, agriculture, trade, and within broad areas of concern, like, environment, economics, socio-cultural aspects etc. Now-a-days these compartments have dissolved. This applies in particular to the various global 'crises' that have seized the public concerns, particularly over the past decade. Now, it seems the environmental crisis, the development crisis, the energy crisis or the socio-economic-political crisis is not the separate crises; they all may be routed from a major crisis.

Our planet is passing through a period of dramatic growth and fundamental change. According to UN projection, the 5 billion population of the world could be stabilized between 8 and 14 billion sometime in the present century. Thus, we badly need to make room in a finite environment for another human world. More than 90 per cent of the increase will occur in the poorest countries and 90 per cent of that growth would be held in the already bursting cities of those countries. Now the question is how to tackle this problem?

World Commission on Environment and Development

The World Commission on Environment and Development first met in October 1984 and published its Report 900 days later, in April 1987. Over those 900 days the world witnessed the following major man-made disasters:

- The drought-triggered environment-development crisis in Africa peaked putting 36 million people at risk and death of approximately a million.
- A leak from a pesticides factory in Bhopal, India, caused death of more than 2,000 people and blinded and long-term injury over 200,000 more.
- Liquid gas tanks exploded in Mexico City killing 1,000 and leaving thousands more homeless.
- The Chernobyl nuclear reactor explosion sent nuclear fallout across the Europe increasing the risks of cancer for future human generations.
- Agricultural chemicals, solvents, and mercury flowed into the Rhine River during a warehouse fire in Switzerland killing millions of different varieties of fish, flora and fauna, and threatening drinking water in the Federal Republic of Germany and the Netherlands.

- An estimated 60 million people died of diarrhea and diseases related to unsafe drinking water and malnutrition of which most of the victims were children in the third world.

The mainspring of economic growth is based on introduction of new technology, and while this technology offers the potential for slowing the dangerously rapid consumption of finite resources, it also entails high risks including new forms of pollution and the introduction to the planet of new variations of life forms that could change evolutionary pathways. Meanwhile, the industries most heavily reliant on environmental resources and most heavily polluting are growing most rapidly in the developing world, where there is both more urgency for growth and less capacity to minimize damaging side effects. These related changes have locked the global economy and global ecology together in new ways.

The Concept of Sustainable Development

Humanity has the ability to make development sustainable to ensure that it meets the needs of the present without compromising the ability of future generations to meet their own needs. The concept of sustainable development does imply limits—not absolute limits but limitations imposed by the present state of technology and social organization on environmental resources and by the ability of the biosphere to absorb the effects of human activities. But technology and social organization can be both managed and improved to make way for a new era of economic growth. The Commission (WCED, 1984) believes that widespread poverty is no longer inevitable. Poverty is not only an evil in itself, but sustainable development requires meeting the basic needs of all and extending to all the opportunity to fulfill their aspirations for a better life. A world in which poverty is endemic will always be prone to ecological and other catastrophes.

Meeting essential needs requires not only a new era of economic growth for nations in which the majority are poor, but an assurance that those poor get their fair share of the resources required to sustain that growth. Such equity would be aided by political systems that secure effective citizens participation in decision making and by greater democracy in international decision-making.

Sustainable global development requires that those who are more affluent should adopt life-styles within the planet's ecological means. Furthermore, rapidly growing populations can increase the pressure on resources and can make it slow the rise in living standards. Thus, sustainable development can only be pursued if population size and growth are in harmony with the changing productive potential of the ecosystem.

Yet in the end, sustainable development is not a fixed state of harmony, but rather a process of change in which the exploitation of resources, the direction of investments, the orientation of technological development, and institutional change are made consistent with future as well as present needs. We do not pretend that the process is easy or straightforward. Painful choices have to be made. In the final analysis, sustainable development must rest mostly on political will.

The Policy Directions

The Commission (WCED, 1984) has focused its attention in the areas of population, food security, the loss of species and genetic resources, energy, industry, and human settlements—realizing that all of these are connected and cannot be treated in isolation one from another. This contains only a few of the Commission's many recommendations:

Population and Human Resources

In many parts of the world, the population is growing at rates that cannot be sustained by available environmental resources, at rates that are outstripping any reasonable expectations of improvements in housing, health care, food security, or energy supplies.

The issue is not just numbers of people, but how those numbers relate to available resources. Thus, the 'population problem' must be dealt with in part by efforts to eliminate mass poverty, in order to assure more equitable access to resources, and by education to improve human potential to manage those resources.

Food Security: Sustaining the Potential

Growth in world cereal production has steadily outstripped world population growth. Yet each year there are more people in the world who do not get enough food. Global agriculture has the potential to grow enough food for all, but food is often not available where it is needed.

Species and Ecosystems: Resources for Development

The planet's species are under stress. There is a growing scientific consensus that species are disappearing at rates never before witnessed on the planet, although there is also controversy over those rates and the risks they entail. Yet there is still time to halt this process.

The diversity of species is necessary for the normal functioning of ecosystems and the biosphere as a whole. The genetic material in wild species contributes billions of dollars yearly to the world economy in the form of improved crop species, new drugs and medicines, and raw materials for industry. But utility aside, there are also moral, ethical, cultural, aesthetic, and purely scientific reasons for conserving wild beings.

Energy: Choices for Environment and Development

A safe and sustainable energy pathway is crucial to sustainable development; we have not yet found it. Rates of increase in energy use have been declining. However, the industrialization, agricultural development, and rapidly growing populations of developing nations will need much more energy. Today, the average person in an industrial market economy uses more than 80 times as much energy as someone in Sub-Saharan Africa. Thus, any realistic global energy scenario must provide for substantially increased primary energy use by developing countries.

To bring developing countries' energy use up to industrialized country levels by the year 2025 would require increasing present global energy use by a factor of five. The planetary ecosystem could not stand this, especially if the increases were based on non-renewable fossil fuels. Threats of global warming and acidification of the environment most probably rule out even a doubling of energy use bared on present mixes of primary sources.

Industry: Producing More with Less

The world manufactures seven times more goods today than it did as recently as 1950. Given population growth rates, a five to tenfold increase in manufacturing output will be needed just to raise developing world consumption of manufactured goods to industrialized world levels by the time population growth rates level of next century.

Experience in the industrialized nations has proved that anti-pollution technology has been cost-effective in terms of health, property, and environmental damage avoided, and that it has made many industries more profitable by making them more resource-efficient. While economic growth has continued, the consumption of raw materials has held steady or even declined, and new technologies offer further efficiencies.

The Urban Challenge

By the turn of the century, almost half of humanity will live in cities; the world of the 21st century will be a largely urban world. Over only 65 years, the developing world's urban population has increased tenfold, from around 100 million in 1920 to 1 billion today. In 1940, one person in 100 lived in a city of 1 million or more inhabitants; by 1980, one in 10 lived in such a city. Between 1985 and the year 2000, Third World cities could grow by another three-quarter of a billion people. This suggests that the developing world must, over the next few years, increase by 65 per cent of its capacity to produce and manage its urban infrastructure, services, and shelter merely to maintain today's often extremely inadequate conditions.

Thus, the sustainable development debate is based on the assumption that societies need to manage three types of capital, economic, social, and natural, which may be non-substitutable and whose consumption might be irreversible. Major Social and Economic Dimensions of Agenda 21 (World Commission on Environment and Development, 1984) are:

i. International cooperation to accelerate sustainable development in developing countries and related domestic policies;
ii. Combating poverty;
iii. Changing consumption patterns;
iv. Demographic dynamics and sustainability;
v. Protecting and promoting human health condition;
vi. Promoting sustainable human settlement development.

Education for Sustainable Development

The recognition of the key role of Education and Communication in enabling and enhancing sustainable development came later. Originally perceived as education about sustainability, it is being increasingly recognized, through the influence of Agenda 21 and the World Summit on Sustainable Development, as more than the dissemination of knowledge. Education at all levels can shape the world of tomorrow, equipping individuals and societies with the skills, perspectives, knowledge and values to live and work in a sustainable manner.

Education for sustainable development (ESD) is a dynamic concept that utilizes all aspects of public awareness, education and training to create or enhance an understanding of the linkages among the issues of sustainable development. Education for sustainable development is a vision of education that seeks to balance human and economic well-being with cultural traditions and respect for the earth's natural resources.

ESD applies trans-disciplinary educational methods and approaches to develop an ethic for lifelong learning; fosters respect for human needs that are compatible with sustainable use of natural resources and the needs of the planet; and nurtures a sense of global solidarity.

Pursuing sustainable development through education requires educators and learners to reflect critically on their own communities; identify non-viable elements in their lives; and explore tensions among conflicting values and goals. ESD brings a new motivation to learning as pupils become empowered to develop and evaluate alternative visions of a sustainable future and to work to collectively fulfill these visions.

Chapter 36 of Agenda 21, adopted at the Earth Summit in Rio (1992), is devoted to 'Promoting Education, Public Awareness and Training'. It identifies four major thrusts of Education for Sustainable Development:

i. Promotion and Improvement of Basic Education,
ii. Re-orienting Existing Education at all Levels to Address Sustainable Development,
iii. Developing Public Understanding and Awareness of Sustainability, and
iv. Training.

ESD is a vision of education that seeks to empower people to assume responsibility for creating a sustainable future. Central to ESD is the concept of culture as an essential underlying theme. It has been acknowledged that there is no single route to sustainable development. Further, it is clear that understandings of, and visions for, sustainability will be different for each of us and that we will need to work together to negotiate the process of achieving sustainability. There are many different stakeholders in sustainable development (i.e., governments, businesses, educational institutions, media, youths, etc). Each of these sectors has a different vision of sustainable development and how it can contribute. Some are interested in environmental preservation and protection; some have economic development interests while others may be more interested in social development. In addition, how each nation, cultural group and individual views sustainable development will depend on its own values. The values held in a society help define how personal decisions are made and how national legislation is written (UNESCO, 2005).

The challenge is to bring these different stakeholders together so that they may collaborate in partnerships to find a balance between their interests and priorities. Various approaches to ESD encourage people to understand the complexities of, and synergies between, the issues threatening planetary sustainability and understand and assess their own values and those of the society in which they live in the context of sustainability.

Basic Characteristics of Education for Sustainable Development

If ESD is to be an effective tool for engaging people in negotiating a sustainable future, making decisions and acting on them, it must first address the way we think about sustainable development and about education in general. Essential to ESD are the following skills (Adapted from Tilbury, D. and Wortman, D. (2004):

i. *Envisioning*—being able to imagine a better future. The premise is that if we know where we want to go, we will be better able to work out how to get there.
ii. *Critical thinking and reflection*—learning to question our current belief systems and to recognize the assumptions underlying our knowledge, perspective and opinions. Critical thinking skills help people learn to examine economic, environmental, social and cultural structures in the context of sustainable development.
iii. *Systemic thinking*—acknowledging complexities and looking for links and synergies when trying to find solutions to problems.
iv. *Building partnerships*—promoting dialogue and negotiation, learning to work together.
v. *Participation in decision-making*—empowering people.

These skills should be learnt and applied according to the cultural contexts of different groups and stakeholders.

The UN Decade of Education for Sustainable Development (DESD)

Director-General of UNESCO, Koïchiro Matsuura on the occasion of the launching of the Decade of Education for Sustainable Development (DESD) in New York on 1 March, 2005 said, "The ultimate goal of the Decade is that education for sustainable development must be more than just a slogan. It must be a concrete reality for all of us—individuals, organization, governments—in all our daily decisions and actions, so as to promise a sustainable planet and a safer world to our children, our grandchildren and their descendants. The principles of sustainable development must find themselves in children's schooling, higher education, non-formal education and community-based learning activities. This means that education will have to change so that it addresses the social, economic, cultural and environmental problems that we face in the 21st century."

Education for Sustainable Development is a dynamic and expansive undertaking that **envisions a world** where every person has the chance to benefit from educational opportunities and to learn the lifestyles, behaviours and values necessary to create a sustainable future. There are two specific goals for the DESD (2005-1014):

i. To provide an opportunity for refining and promoting the vision of, and transition to, sustainable development—through all forms of education, public awareness and training,

ii To give an enhanced profile to the important role of education and learning in sustainable development.

The objectives of the DESD are:

i. To facilitate networking linkages, exchange and interaction among stakeholders in ESD;
ii. To foster increased quality of teaching and learning in ESD;
iii. To help countries make progress towards and attain the Millennium Development Goals through ESD efforts;
iv. To provide countries with new opportunities to incorporate ESD into education reform efforts.

From the above discussions a schema for the ESD can be constructed in the following way for further studies:

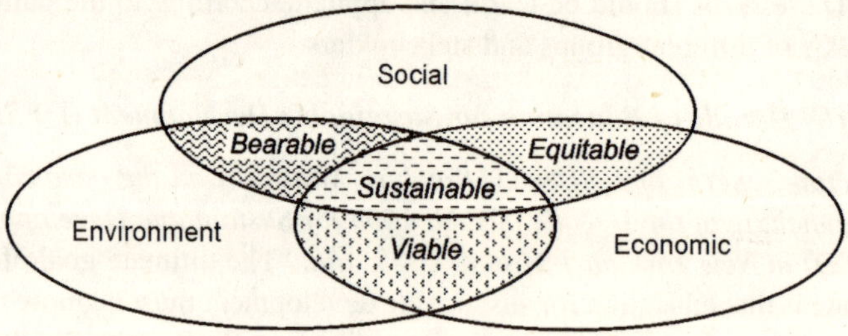

Fig. 4.1: Schema of Education for Sustainable Development

Education, Sustainable Development and Quality Education

In defining what 'quality education' means in the context of educating for sustainability, UNESCO calls for the "reorientation of education systems, policies and practices in order to empower everyone, young and old, to make decisions and act in Social, Environmental and Economic intermixed sectors having Bearable socio-environmental, Viable Environ-economic and Equitable Socio-Economic joint sectors on the basis of culturally appropriate, locally relevant and psychologically acceptable ways to redress the problems that threaten our common future." Thus,

Education is a prerequisite for education for sustainable development. Achieving sustainable development requires—

i. Recognition of the challenges,
ii. Collective responsibility and constructive partnership,
iii. Acting with determination,
iv. The indivisibility of human dignity.

Education provides the skills for—Learning to know, Learning to live together, Learning to do and Learning to be. It not only provides scientific and technical skills, it also provides the motivation, justification, and social support for pursuing and applying them. The international community now strongly believes that we need to foster—through education—the values, behaviour and lifestyles required for our sustainable future.

REFERENCES

Daly, H.E. (1973). *Towards a Steady State Economy.* San Francisco: Freeman.

Daly, H.E. (1991). *Steady-State Economics* (2nd ed.). Washington, D.C.: Island Press.

Hasna, A.M. (2007). "Dimensions of Sustainability". *Journal of Engineering for Sustainable Development: Energy, Environment, and Health* 2(1): 47-57.

Meadows, D., Meadows, D.L., Randers, J., and Behrens, W. (1971). *The Limits to Growth.* New York: Universe Books.

Smith, Charles; Rees, Gareth (1998). *Economic Development.* 2nd edition. Basingstoke: Macmillan.

Stivers, R. (1976). *The Sustainable Society: Ethics and Economic Growth.* Philadelphia: Westminster Press.

United Nations (1987). *Report of the World Commission on Environment and Development.* General Assembly Resolution 42/187, 11 December 1987. Retrieved: 2007-04-12

UCN (2006). *The Future of Sustainability: Re-thinking Environment and Development in the Twenty-first Century.* Report of the IUCN Renowned Thinkers Meeting, 29-31 January, 2006; http://cmsdata.iucn.org/downloads/iucn

United Nations Division for Sustainable Development (2007). *Documents: Sustainable Development Issues* Retrieved: 2007-05-12.

Will Allen (2007).*"Learning for Sustainability: Sustainable Development."*

World Health Organization (2005). *World Summit Outcome Document,* 15 September, 2005.

5

Education System in Pakistan and Sustainable Human Resource Development

Hafeez-Ur-Rehmanchaudhry, M. Saifullah Chaudhry and *Md. Amjad Kavesh*

Education always remains an indispensable tool for achieving sustainability. The functions of the educational institutions are to develop the people physically, mentally, psychologically, socially and spiritually. It improves and promotes the economic social, political and cultural life of the nation. In Pakistan, the low primary school enrolment, the high school dropout, extremely limited formal vocational and skill training system, and continues dismal performance made country "off-track" against the Millenium Development Goal 2 (MDG 2). These signs are symptoms of a problem and not the problem itself. The large number of out of school children sooner or later enter the informal economy as child labour with limited wages. The increasing number of poor and working poor in Pakistan may be finding themselves caught in an unending and vicious cycle of poverty. Pakistani society appears to be dividing in two broad categories, 'haves' and 'have not', the bourgeoisie and the proletariat and possibly on a collision course.

The Background

The institution of education remains imperative throughout the human history. In primitive times, man took the help of informal kind of educational institution in order to pass his experience and skills to younger generation. One possible interpretation for the cave painting by Cro-Magnon man about 30,000 years ago in the caves of Europe is that they were by the senior members of society to transmit information, hunting strategies and at some extent, very simple value structure to junior members. In modern time, educational institutions are not only feeding the market place but they allow people to have information on different kind of social dramas, vision on the globalization and is strengthening the existing value system. The value system adopted and encouraged by any society is indoctrinated to youth through the socialization process. Within the complex process of socialization, formal and informal education stands first, which not only legitimately propagate the existing value system to youth but mold their attitude in such manner so they may respect it. The education systems in any state practicing to control the deviant forms of behaviour which may be considered illicit for the development of social order and mold it to an extent so it may appear to be the prosperous identity of that particular nation. Uniformity, social solidarity and resistance against the irregularities in order to provide the rational reasoning of existing phenomenon is the chief objective of educational institution throughout the modern world.

In order to trace the history of the education for sustainable development, first time in 1987, UN General Assembly recognized the parallel concept of education and its support to the sustainable development. From 1987 to 1992 the concept gets more matured as the discussion on different levels has been made to discover the future dimension in this regard. Unlike most education movements, the Education for sustainable development was initiated by the people outside the education community. In the modern era it is being recognized that current economic development trends are not the actual form of sustainability but the education and awareness to general public lead a society towards sustainability. Although there remains the strong debate about the sustainable development among the scholars of all disciplines and the question whether the true sustainable development can be attained or not, remains unsolved. Charies Hopkins and Rosalyn McKeown noted that,

> "We can rapidly create a laundry list of problems—inefficient use of energy, lack of water conservation, pollution, abuses of human rights, overuse of personal transportation, consumerism, etc. However, we should not chide ourselves because we do not have a clear definition of sustainability; many truly great concepts of the human world, such as democracy and justice, are hard to define and have multiple expressions in cultures around the world." (*Hopkins & McKeown*, 2002, p. 13)

To attain the goals of sustainability within any nation, education in all perspectives—formal, non-formal and informal—remain vital. Formal education cannot only teach the people everything about living or working and does not carry the responsibility for sustainable development but the non-formal educational sectors (NGOs, Public Health Educators, Agricultural Extension agents etc.) and the informal educational sectors (media, socialization process etc.) all work combined to achieve the well define goals of sustainability.

In Pakistan before contextualizing the overall discourse of education, it is important to regard the gender gap, where the girls are discouraged at all levels of education. The government is the largest provider of education while private educational institutions are playing their part to run some kind of business industry. The Western standard education (English medium schools and colleges) are creating a huge class shift and available to those who can cope with the heavy fee structure, while most of the government educational institution (Urdu medium school and colleges) are available to the majority of masses. In order to meet the modern trends and the need of market places, the concept of private academy tuitions is growing in all major provinces of the country.

Pakistan has huge educational system with about 2,27,791 registered educational institutions from pre-primary, primary, middle and secondary schools to various types colleges and universities. Although, it is spoken by many policy makers and written down in most of the annual educational reports that basic education is the birthright of every child within the country, but the on practical grounds the situation is not so. The education standards within the country is shaped in such an manner that 16 years of time and money investment make a boy eligible to enter in the market place with meaning share in society.

The 16 years of formal education which appears to be so long for poor parents, also provides many of them insight of technical education. The proposition of technical education remains helpful in two important ways, first it allows future economic security to the poor parents (as it is obvious that in the growing trend of unemployment within the country, the technically employed people never become jobless) who are spending a reasonable share of their income on their children education and secondly technical education open the opportunities of overseas employment (where the high-valued foreign currency become the reason of long term family development). So, in the longer-term interest of promoting moderation and democratic values in Pakistan, and in improving the socioeconomic status of its people, sector-wide reform of the education system appears vital.

Child Labour, Marxist Perspective and Dysfunctional Education System

The Marxist perspective provides a unique theoretical foundation to discuss conflicting aspects of society regarding the child labour discussion in developing countries like Pakistan. Marx viewed people both as producers and the products of society. People make society themselves by their own actions. Marx built his idea of history on the premises of dialectic. The dialectical movement represents the conflict of contradictions. It is the conflict that forms the basis of dynamic principles and source of change. The tension between incompatible forces leads to change. This struggle eventually results in collision of incompatible forces. Consequently, a sudden change creates a new set of rules at a higher level of development. The dialectic process starts again as a contradiction between a new set of forces begins. Marx argued that the source of change embedded, in particular, in the contradictions of the economic system and the society in general. His focus on economic factors meant that this view became known as 'dialectical materialism'. (Marx, K. and Engels, F., 1971)

For Marx the two-class model was the crux of his dialectic of social change. He postulated structure of all societies in simplified terms of two-classes, the ruling class and the subject class. The ruling class, the bourgeoisie, has the power due to its ownership and control over means of production. The subject class, the proletariat, is powerless because of its lack of ownership of means of production. The conflict between these two classes originates because the labour of the subject class produces results that are solely appropriated by the ruling class (*ibid*, 1971).

The absence of a well-functioning school education for all children compel parents to rely on alternative means of informal human resource development (for example, informal skills training through an *Ustaad-Shagirid* arrangement) that may only expand the proletariat class. School education in Pakistan has been primarily designed in such a way that it requires at least 16 years of time investment and corresponding financial resources to become eligible for a meaningful share in the society (in terms of gainful employment). However, even this long-term investment may not be enough to develop ownership and control means of production, and in fact children of the proletariat (working classes) continue to be denied meaningful economic engagement in the process. Thus, such a bleak future prospects compel poor parents to participate and create a culture of child labour that may provide some solace to the proletariat.

However, dialectical materialism may perpetuate the conflict between these working classes (proletariat) and the ruling class (bourgeoisie). It is the bourgeoisie that continue to occupy the decision-making role in resource allocation or lack of it, for social services like education.

In this theoretical backdrop the following section attempts to situate the discussion around education and child labour in the South Asian region.

South Asian Context on Education and Child Labour

Traditional and non-industrialized societies, like South Asian, continued to accept the presence of children in the world of work. Before British colonization of India (almost all of South Asia) the concept of *Maddarrass* (School for religious teachings and to learn languages) and *Sansikrit* College (for Hindu students) were prevalent during the Mughal Era. Moreover, children would acquire various skills in agriculture, blacksmith, goldsmith, carpentry, construction, weaving, pottery, painting, architecture, and commerce through apprenticeship by entering into the world of work at an early age. However, it was the British who introduced the formal school system and developed certain curriculum to train children for future jobs suitable to the functioning of the colonial system in India. More importantly, the British succeeded in replacing the vernacular languages (Persian, Arabic, Urdu and Sansikrit) with the English language as a medium of instruction in school and colleges to the resentment of the locals. It was "Lord Macualay (who) succeeded in introducing English language as medium of instruction instead of establishing national education system". (Bokhari, 1986, p. 92)

Although the British introduced the school system in South Asia it was never a blanket system catering to all children, that is, compulsory education. Even today both India and Pakistan have not made primary education compulsory in real terms nor have they reversed the British colonial policy with respect to primary school education. Weiner and Noman (1995) indicated that before World War I, the Indian National Congress introduced a private bill in the central legislature in New Delhi demanding compulsory primary education. This bill received support from some of the leaders of Indian National Congress and the Muslim League, however majority of the members of the Central Legislature, most officials, and representatives of princely states opposed it.

The crux of the argument against compulsory primary education has been that "poverty forces children to drop out of school to find employment to augment the income of their families. It is an argument widely subscribed to by all political groups (Weiner & Noman, 1995, p. 186)". Moreover, another argument has been that education would make the poor unsuited for boring manual work that society requires. However, the Prussian government found an alternative solution "which emphasized vocational training for working class children. The children of the poor were compelled to attend the Volksschule, where they were taught skills that would enable them to remain in the working class. It was a policy that probably contributed to the technical quality of German Products (Weiner & Noman, 1991, p. 116)". In other words, due to a variety of reasons, marginalized segments of society in South Asia could not benefit from school education. Thus the traditional concept of children going directly into the adult world through the path of apprenticeship is still in vogue.

Behera (2007) linked the problem of child labour with poverty, insufficient educational system and employment. She states, "A highly visible problem in recent decades in South Asia is child labour. Many children work either as unskilled or as apprentices in skilled production. While unskilled child labour is due to the problem of poverty and infrastructural bottlenecks in education and employment, apprenticeship is a complex system within which skills and ethical training are imparted and future employment guaranteed. Children, working as apprentices in trades such as weaving and pottery work in domestic settings, are not neglected or abused although they certainly are not given the separate spaces, resources, and consumer goods taken as normative in the West."

She further pointed out that child labour is both the cause and consequence of poverty. However, she also acknowledges the role of cultural norms in the prevalence of child labour. "Tradition and culture also play a role, and perceptions of the nature of childhood and the role and responsibilities of children towards their elders and siblings often decide whether a child is sent to school or into labour. In some societies this is especially true for girl children" (Behera, 2007).

With this brief historical background it is pertinent to critically review the nature of human resource development system presently prevalent in Pakistan and how it becomes a source of pushing families to send children into labour instead.

Human Resource Development System and Child Labour

The human resource development system in Pakistan is designed in a vertical manner with the assumption that all children would at least attain ten years of school education (matriculation) before deciding (primarily by parents) on their future course of action. Therefore the horizontal linkages between school education and skills training providers are not available for school children before the 10th grade. After ten years of school education, the subsequent six years education of college and university is also well established as a possible course of action. Nonetheless, education is generally viewed in terms of the following bench marks[1] :

No.	*Level*	*Numbers of Years*
1	Primary School	Five year of school education. Grade 1 to 5
2	Middle School	Three year of school education, after Primary school
3	Matriculation (High School)	Two years of school education, after Middle School
4	Intermediate	Two years of college education, after Matriculation
5	Bachelors	Two years of college education, after Intermediate
6	Masters	Two years of university education, after Bachelors

This human resource development system offers two broad courses of action for students completing their Intermediate; that is either to opt for university education or professional colleges (medical, engineering and so on). In other words, after intermediate (12 years of education) qualifying students can choose to go to professional colleges (spend four to five years) or to do a university degree (4 years). This link of school education with professional colleges and University is well established and visible to communities.

School education is also linked to technical and vocational education. However this option is available to a limited number of school children and has weak linkages with the formal school education system. Students after completing matriculation can opt for skills and vocational training and after doing their Intermediate can also choose technical training. However, these linkages are not clearly known to families, particularly those who send their children to work. The following Figure 5.1 depicts the broader architect of the formal human resource mechanism available in the country:

For many families the purpose of education is primarily to ensure their children find gainful employment. In general, 16 or 14 years of formal education a long-term investment for children, and most poor parents consider it a difficult proposition. The human resource development model primarily relies on formal school education with vertical linkages to college and subsequently with university or

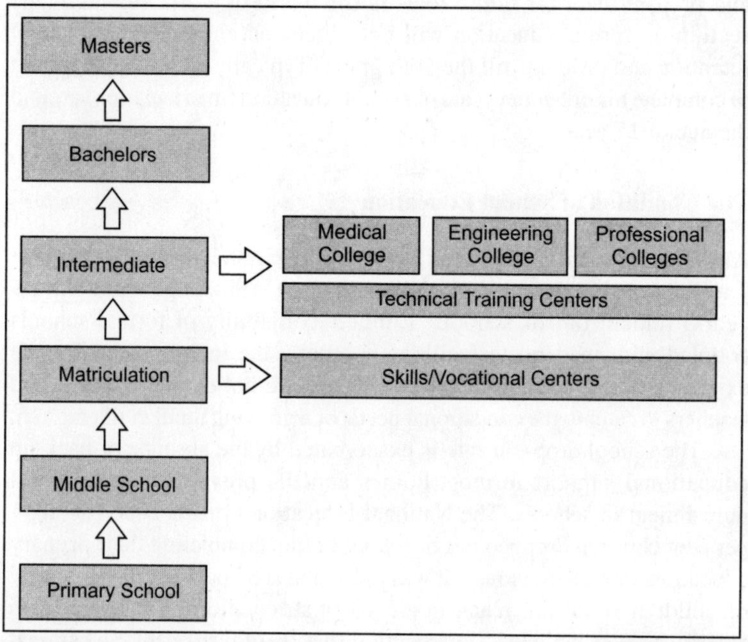

Fig. 5.1: Broad Architect of Human Resource Development System in Pakistan[2]

professional colleges. At the stage of moving into professional colleges, the system becomes extremely competitive and expensive. Moreover, for poorer segments of society, the system does not guarantee automatic transfer from school/colleges to employment. At the same time, there is also no guarantee that a student who reaches a higher level of education, for example to university degree, would immediately secure employment after graduation.

This human resource development system demands heavy investment of time (at least ten years) and financial resources from the family to enable their children to enter the world of work for formal employment. Even these ten years of education would not enable a person skilled enough to find meaningful employment. At best a Matriculate, if lucky, may find employment in the private sector that would offer remunerations equivalent to the minimum wage, that is, rupees 7000[3] per month and on a precarious contract. Such a person would not easily find better employment.

The next section will present a critical view of the human resource system, consisting of both education and skills training streams, depicting how effectively or otherwise it enroll and retain children within its fold and prepare them for future roles in the world of work. However, the section on formal education will only focus on enrolment and school retention and dropouts till the 10th grade. Typically a child is supposed to complete his or her ten years of school education (matriculation) around the age of 15 years.

The Condition of School Education

As discussed earlier, the United Nations in Pakistan indicates that almost 7 million of the estimated 19 million primary school age children (5-9 years) remain out of school.[4] Limited availability of formal schools coupled with inadequate facilities is among the major causes for the existence of out of school children. There are not enough schools and teachers to cater to the educational needs of a growing number of children.

The school drop-out rate is exacerbated by the absence of back-up educational support in most homes and the prevalence of corporal punishment in schools. The National Education Census 2006 found 31 per cent children dropped out of school before completing their primary education, though previously it was estimated at 50 per cent. The majority of children could not reach grade 10 (matriculation). These statistics clearly support the general perception that the government educational infrastructure is inadequate, inefficient and largely unsuccessful in catering to the educational needs of Pakistani children.

However, the progress of Pakistan against the Millennium Development Goal 2 (MDG), Universal Primary Education, is dismal and country is 'off-track', as it will not achieve 100 per cent NER, it still has 50 per cent drop-out at primary education level; literacy ratio is at 57 per cent much short of 88 per cent target by 2015. Thus there seems considerable shortfall in achieving the MDG targets for Goal 2 (Pakistan Millennium Development Goals 2010; p. 3). The yearly education statistics confirms this state of affair.

The Table 5.1 presents ten years statistics of government school enrolment and retention from 1st grade to 10th grade.

The table indicates almost half of the children dropped out of school before completing primary education. The shaded boxes indicate the retention from 1st grade to 10th grade of one batch of all government school children. In 1997-98, 2.41 million children who were enrolled in 1st grade were reduced to 1.1 million (46% retention) in 6th grade, and in 2006-07 only to 0.56 million (23% retention) were left in 10th grade. Conversely, the school dropout, from the initial enrolment of 2.41 million

Table 5.1: School Enrolment and Retention by Year and Class (1997-98 to 2006-07)

Class	*1997-98*	*1998-99*	*1999-00*	*2000-01*	*2001-02*	*2002-03*	*2003-04*	*2004-05*	*2005-06*	*2006-07*
Class 1	2.41 (100%)	2.49	2.68	2.77	2.69	2.83	2.77	2.96	3.26	3.30
Class 2	1.98	1.79	1.93	2.05	2.16	2.17	2.12	2.29	2.55	2.65
Class 3	1.77	1.55	1.67	1.72	1.83	1.89	1.95	1.99	2.14	2.25
Class 4	1.62	1.36	1.53	1.52	1.59	1.62	1.77	1.85	1.94	1.93
Class 5	1.42	1.31	1.31	1.34	1.35 (56%)	1.39	1.53	1.60	1.68	1.60
Class 6	1.20	1.20	1.16	1.05	1.10	1.1 (46%)	1.16	1.24	1.38	1.38
Class 7	0.99	1.01	1.01	0.94	0.93	0.95	1.01	1.04	1.17	1.19
Class 8	0.84	0.87	0.90	0.86	0.87	0.87	0.91	0.92	1.00	1.04
Class 9	0.71	0.72	0.75	0.71	0.71	0.71	0.75	0.75	0.80	1.02
Class 10	0.55	0.58	0.56	0.54	0.53	0.54	0.59	0.64	0.65	0.56 (23%)

in 1st grade, was 54 per cent at 6th grade and dropouts rose drastically to 77 per cent by the time the same batch reached 10th grade. Clearly, it indicates, among other factors, parents and students lack of faith in the system of school education.

Figure 5.2 presents Extracted Time-Series Data About School Enrolment at Primary, Middle and High School Levels. This time series data covers the period of 11 years from 1996-97 till 2006-7 and was compiled by the Federal Bureau of Statistics (FBS), Government of Pakistan. Over the eleven year period the enrolment at primary level has increased from 15.4 million in 1996-97 to 24.5 million in 2006-07. However, the enrolment at middle school level only moved from 3.73 to 5.37 million during the same period of eleven years. This also indicated a high drop out of children while moving from primary to middle levels of school. This drop-out rate becomes more pronounced as high school enrolment has moved from 1.52 to 2.31 million during the same period.

In Pakistan, the private sector also plays a significant role in catering to the educational needs of children. During the last two decades there has been a rapid growth of private schools catering to those segments of the societies that could afford it. These schools are now visible in large and small cities, and even in rural towns. Many of these private schools are perceived as a means to receive quality education for children—a service that is believed to be eroding in government schools. The general perception about government schools as the provider of quality education has deteriorated over the last couple of decades. Resultantly, the demand for private schools has risen.

This has resulted in children from middle and upper middle classes to get enrolled in private schools. Largely, the children from poorer segments of society are enrolled in government schools. However, there are private schools that cater to people from a low income bracket too. Entrepreneurial teacher would convert one or two room of his/her house into a tiny school. He would engage one or two more teachers. The fee structure is low and only activity is teaching the children who would enroll from the neighborhood. Table 5.2 provides the number of children enrolled both in public and private sector schools. It is important to note that the private sector caters to 37 per cent children at the pre-primary, and roughly close to 30 per cent at primary, middle and high school levels. However, school dropouts are observed in both public and private sectors.

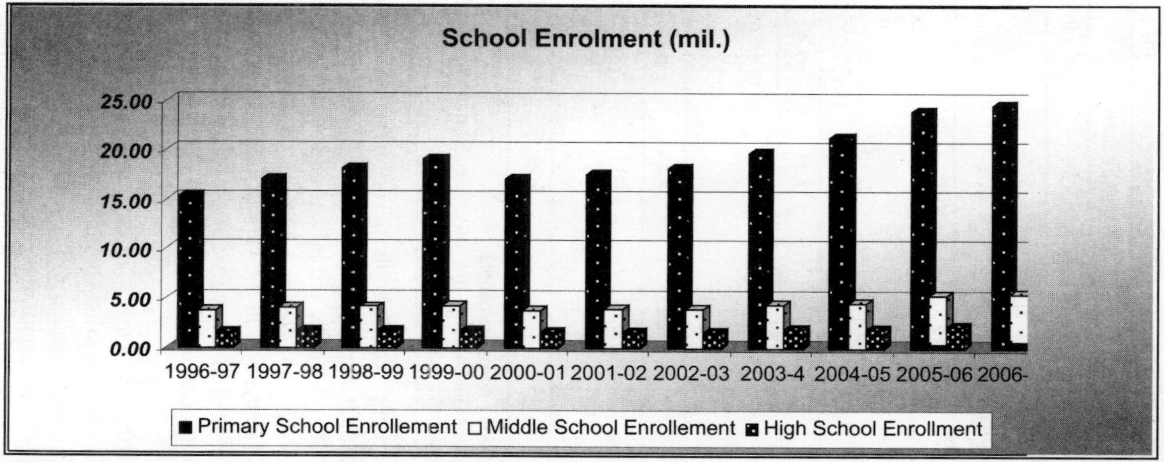

School Enrollment (in millions)

Categories	1996-97	1997-98	1998-99	1999-00	2000-01	2001-02	2002-03	2003-4	2004-05	2005-06	2006-07
Primary School Enrollement	15.40	17.06	18.17	19.15	17.14	17.53	18.22	19.78	21.33	23.97	24.59
Middle School Enrollement	3.73	4.03	4.10	4.11	3.76	3.82	3.92	4.32	4.55	5.26	5.37
High School Enrollment	1.52	1.66	1.70	1.73	1.57	1.57	1.59	1.80	1.88	2.13	2.31

Fig. 5.2: Enrolment in Primary, Middle and High Schools (1996-2007)

Table 5.2: School Enrolment in Public and Private Schools (2006-07)

				mil
Institution Type		*Enrolment by State*		
		Boys	*Girls*	*Total*
Pre-Primary	Pubic	2.50	Z05	4.56
	Other Pubic	0.05	0.05	0I10
	Private	152	1.25	2.77
	Total	**4.08**	**3.34**	**7.42**
Primary	Pubic	6.69	5.04	11.73
	Other Pubic	0.14	0.13	0£7
	Private	2.80	2.25	5.04
	Total	**9.62**	**7.41**	**17.04**
Middle	Pubic	Z18	1.43	3.62
	Other Pubic	0.05	0.05	0.10
	Private	0.89	0.76	1.65
	Total	**3.13**	**2.24**	**5.37**
High	Pubic	0.97	0.60	1.57
	Other Pubic	0.03	0.03	0.05
	Private	0.37	0.32	0.69
	Total	**1.36**	**0.95**	**2.31**

i. Mosque Schools are included in primary schools.
ii. Other Public Sectors Means institutions run by other than Ministry of Education or Provincial/Regional Education Departments.

Despite the rapid growth of private schools, the difference of school enrolments at primary, middle and high school levels indicate the continued limited capacity of both public and private education systems in the country to enroll and retain children in schools. As argued earlier too, most school dropouts happen within the various levels of primary school education and also soon after grade five. A predominant number of the school going children move out of school and could potentially enter the world of work.

Various factors are attributed to this high degree of school dropouts. In 2003-04, the Ministry of Education commissioned a longitudinal study on access and equity in basic education. These series of studies are being carried out in fourteen representative districts across the four provinces of the country. So far only two studies have been published and the results of these studies provide useful insights into the phenomenon of low enrolment and dropout of children at the primary school level. In

2005, the Ministry of Education's study on Access and Equity in Basic Education presented useful insights as well. (Shami & Hussain, 2005) The study, while exploring the reasons for low school enrolment, indicated that in all the fourteen districts of the samples, only 36 per cent children had access to schools whereas 64 per cent children were out of school or had no access to school at primary level. The study provided many reasons for not enrolling boys in the schools. In the opinion of 65 per cent parents an extra earning member of the family was an important reason of not enrolling boys in school. Moreover, 62 per cent parents were of the view that their children were not interested in getting an education, another 60 per cent thought that their children provided help at home.

The same study of the Ministry of Education also investigated the reasons for high school dropouts, and found that lack of guidance and the educational expenses turned out to be important reasons for a high dropout rate. Other reasons included family size, lack of good teachers and the improper behaviour of teachers. Regarding access to primary schools, this study concluded that "54 per cent children had access to primary schools and 46 per cent had no school facility in the year 2003-04."(Shami & Hussain, 2005) This study of the Ministry of Education identified the following factors as a hindrance to boys' and girls' school enrolment:

- Children (boys and girls) have to provide help at home.
- Schools are not available.
- Schools are at long distance from the children's residence.
- Children are not interested in studies.
- There is no opportunity for further education.
- No security for girls.
- Teachers' harsh behaviour.
- No physical facilities.
- Expensive education.
- Children's sickness.

The question arises, what do all those children who either never get enrolled in schools or drop out during or soon after primary schooling do? Those children who drop out before or after completing primary education often enter the world of work at a young age, sometimes when they are seven or eight years old. If this is the case, then the magnitude of child labour in Pakistan could be exceptionally high.

Before moving forward, it would be useful to have a brief look at the state of technical and vocational education in the country. It would also be helpful to see, within the overall human resource system of the country, how technical and vocational education stream performs its function and how it interacts with the regular education system.

The State of Technical and Vocational Education

In Pakistan, the state of public sector technical and vocational education is of low standard, and the private sector is not well organized either. The lack of visibility of horizontal linkages between government schools and skills and vocational training institutions make school education almost unidirectional. These linkages are non-existent below the matriculation level (grade 10). Schools teachers are not aware of available skills and vocational training centres or trades being taught there. Similarly, the skills and vocational centers never make an attempt to introduce skills/ vocational training to the teachers, school children and their parents as alternative and shorter duration career paths than to professional colleges.

The National Skills Strategy 2009-2013 identifies a limited capacity of technical and vocational training institutes in the country. "There are currently only 315,000 enrolled students across 1,647 technical and vocational education and training institutes in Pakistan. It is quite evident therefore that major changes are necessary to achieve these quantitative targets." (The National Skills Strategy, 2009-2013, 2009, p. 17) However, in 2005-06, the total enrolment at the technical and vocational training centers stood at 238,687 students.

The dearth of these training centers, poor quality of training, coupled with the perceived low social status of these trades makes the existence of these technical and vocational training centers almost invisible. Another reason is that formal higher education, despite all drop-outs still has more students than those in the skills and vocational training centers. "About 314,864 students are enrolled in TVET institutes in Pakistan. In comparison, the enrolment in higher secondary, intermediate and degree colleges is 2.2 million. This means that students in TVET are only 14 per cent of those pursuing general education up to the college level. The proportion falls even further if professional and university education is included," (The National Skills Strategy, 2009-2013, 2009, p. 38)

In many instances, poor families are not aware of the existence of the government's skills and vocational training centers. Where, members of marginalized communities know about these centers, the high admission criteria to these centers exclude the children of the poor from benefiting. Students are required to successfully complete Matriculation or Intermediate to be eligible for admission into the skill and vocational training centers.

However, children from marginalized communities drop out of school during or soon after primary schooling (5 years of education), well before they complete their Matriculation (10 years of education) or Intermediate (12 years of education), which is a prerequisite qualification for admission into these skills and vocational training centers. Resultantly, the skills and vocational training infrastructure are unable to cater to the marginalized and vulnerable groups both in urban and rural areas.

Non-Functioning HRD System and Informal Economy

This section will present the broad contours of the flow of the work force from a formal human resource development (HRD) system. Figure 5.3 (while benefiting from the data presented in the Table 4.1 School Enrolment and Retention by Year and Class) indicates that the majority of children sooner or later dropout from schools and eventually find employment in the informal economy. However, no clear data is available that confirms that all those children who dropout from school and immediately enter into employment. In any case, statistical data from various labour force surveys of Pakistan, as also discussed in section 1.3, continues to confirm the existence of child labour.

Nonetheless, it is presumed that once a child, particularly male, is out of school he would potentially end up in some sort of employment sooner or later. Thus between 1996 and 2007, out of a total 2.41 million children who were in class 1, only 0.53 million children could reach grade 10 (data from Table 5.1). In other words, 1.88 million children, who were probably less than 15 years of age, left formal schools and possibly all were absorbed by the informal economy. Clearly, the supply of child labour is common place as the schools fail to retain children within the HRD system. The formal economy, on the other hand, mostly offers employment to highly educated and skilled manpower. Figure 5.3 makes it clear that large majority of students do not reach to a higher level of educational and technical skills development institutions and thus after dropping out from various classes enter into the informal economy.

Clearly, a large majority of the population in Pakistan remaines illiterate due to non-functioning of the formal human resource development system. In this environment, where many children enter in the world work, the workplace education becomes significant for their development. In developing countries, it is the workplace where benefits of the education affect communities and families. Under the Human Resource Development Perspective, such employers who use child

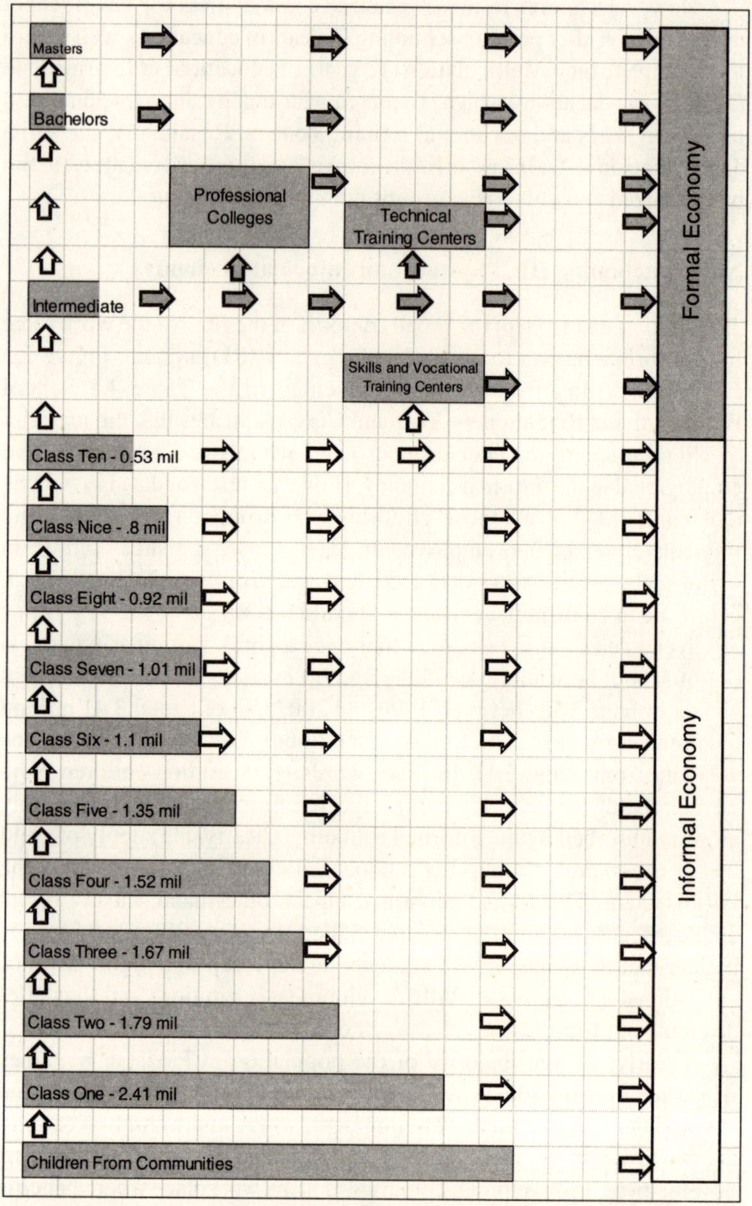

Fig. 5.3: Flow of Work Force From HRD System (1996-97 to 2006-07)

workers and invest in workplace education could be considered as investing in education for their employees (children) but also for their families and the community (Cho & McLean, 2002).

Human Resource Development (HRD) Perspective on Child Labour

There is relatively limited literature that has explored child labour from the human resource development (HRD) perspective. The HRD perspective attempts to look at the issue of child labour as workplace education for the benefit of the community and family (Cho & McLean, 2002). On-the-job training for children is one way of enhancing their skill set and providing them career opportunities. In Kenya, for example, the sector that is creating more employment is in the jua kali—small, roadside businesses. Children in these workplaces perform the role of apprentices and learn skills from skilled people that facilitate children's future employment (McLean, 1996). Moreover, the trade unions in Brazil's gemstone industry set up vocational training centers where child workers are allowed to attend and learn skills. These vocational training centers help children acquire various skills needed to work in the gemstone industry (Myrstad, 1999).

In a study carried out in Bangladesh, Ethiopia, the Philippines, and Central America with three hundred working children, a large majority expressed the desire to combine work with school (Woodhead 1999). These children recognized the high cost of attending school that was required to pay the costs of tuition, books and related costs. Moreover, they also realized the opportunity costs of the potential loss of income by not working. These children also knew about the benefits they could reap from obtaining an education. This study revealed that children do not have the luxury of choice between working and getting an education. Going to school and benefiting from education was desirable, whereas working was a necessity.

In the HRD perspective it is suggested that child labour should be managed rather than eradicated. Since the majority of the population in developing countries is illiterate and children are out of school, workplace education is significant for children's development. "Controlling, not eliminating, child labour will encourage organizations using child workers to develop collaborative relationships with schools so that there will continue to be an inflow of human resource from schools into business. This is a way of making coordinated improvements in work-place education system. Creating such coordinated activities may well be the outcome of community-based organization development" (Budhwani & McLean, 2004, p. 115).

The long-term effect of child labour may not be readily available in the literature. Basu (1998) argues that long terms consequence of child labour is a 'child labour trap', as he assumes that if a child works more his productivity as an adult falls. He presented a model that described that a child labourer "acquires no skills and so as an adult earns very little and has to send his child, in turn, to work full-time. This equilibrium depicts what may be called a child labour trap." (Basu, 1998, pp. 46-47) Alternatively, he describes a situation where "a child goes to school, earns adequately as an adult and so can and does send his child to school. It is a virtuous cycle". (Basu, 1998, pp. 47) For Basu the long-term effects of child labour are negative as his model indicates that these children would have low accumulation of human capital and correspondingly small future incomes.

Nonetheless, parents while keeping in view their limited resources do look at medium term advantages[5] of sending their child to school or to work. They measure the results each of the options would produce. Chamarbagwala (2004) has empirically examined the relationship between rates of return to schooling, child labour, and education in India using individual-level household data from the Employment and Unemployment Schedule of the National Sample Survey Organization (NSSO). Her empirical results "indicate that higher rates of return to education decrease child labour and increase education amongst boys and decrease child labour amongst girls. The rate of return to primary school has a strong impact on boys' participation in child labour and schooling while girls' participation in child labour responds to changes in the rate of return to middle school. (Chamarbagwala, 2004, p. 61)" In order words, if schooling does not offer an adequate return on the investment the poor parents particularly would reject school education to find alternative means of a human resource development mechanism for their children.

Conclusion

In view of data presented, it is evident that the system of available human resource development system in Pakistan is dysfunctional as it fails to cater to the education and training needs of majority of the population. The national education data suggests that 77 per cent nation's children become dropout of school before completing 10th grade of school education, and many even before completing primary education. These out-of-school children are certainly potential child labourers even if they have not entered the world of work. Moreover, Pakistan's efforts against the Millennium Development Goal (MDG) in particular the MDG 2, Universal Primary Education, is now 'off-track', resultantly it will not achieve the target.

This clearly indicates that the educational system has structural faults ranging from its relevance, effectiveness to the investment in the education system to improve it. Clearly, this denies the poor any chance to break out of the vicious cycle of poverty trap. Thus, the ability of poor working classes is compromised to have any meaningful access to society's means of production and resources. This fractured human resource development and consequently dangerously unequal distribution of wealth and resources may further exacerbate, to put it in classical Marxist lexicon, the conflict between the proletariat and the bourgeoisie, with unacceptable consequences for the society.

END NOTES

1. Prepared by the research based on discussions with the officials of Ministry of Education; Higher Education Commission
2. Prepared by the research based on discussions with the officials of Ministry of Education; Higher Education Commission; and Technical Training Providers
3. During 2010-2011, the minimum wage in Pakistan was ₹ 7000.
4. Joint programme Document on Education, One UN programme signed by the UN Pakistan and Ministry of Education in 2009,
5. Pakistan Education Statistics 2006-07", Published by Academy of Education Planning and Management, Ministry of Education, 2008, Islamabad (http://aepam.edu.pk) p. 32.
6. This data is extracted from the Social Surveys of the Federal Bureau of Statistics, Government of Pakistan (http://www.statpak.gov.pk/depts/fbs/statistics/social_statistics/education.pdf)
7. Pakistan Education Statistics 2006-07. (http://aepam.edu.pk)
8. For example, parents chief concerns is that will their child would be able to become financial independent in next seven or eight years.

REFERENCES

Basu, K. (1998). *Child Labour: Causes, Consequences and Cure, with Remarks on International Labour Standards*, The World Bank: World Bank Policy Research Working Paper No. 2027.

Behera, D.K. (2007). *Childhood in South Asia,* New Delhi: Pearson.

Bokhari, S.S. (1986). *MacualayaurBarei-i-SagheerKaNizam-i-Taleem (Macualy and Education System of South Asia)*, Lahore: Tufail Art Printers

Budhwani, N.N., Wee, B., and McLean, G.N. (2004). Should Child Labour be Eliminated? An HRD Perspective, *Human Resource Development Quarterly*, 15(1).

Chamarbagwala, R.M. (2004). *The Role of Capital-Skill Complementarities in Child Labour and Schooling* (Ph.D. Dissertation), Bloomington: Indiana University.

Cho, E.S., and McLean, G.N. (2002). National human resource development: Korean Case. In U. Pareek, A.M. Osman-Gani, S. Ramnaravan, and T.V. Rao (Ed.), *Human Resource Development in Asia: Trends and Challenges* (pp. 253-260). New Delhi: Oxford & IBH Publishing.

Government of Pakistan (2010). Pakistan Millennium Development Goals

Government of Pakistan (2009). The National Skills Strategy 2009-2013. Published by The National Vocational and Technical Education Commission, Islamabad.

Government of Pakistan (2008). Education for All: Mid-Decade Assessment, Pakistan Country Report 2008. Published by Ministry of Education, Islamabad.

Hopkins, C. and McKeown, R. (2002). Education for Sustainable Development: An International Perspective. In Tilbury, D. *et al.* (ed.) *Education and Sustainability, Responding to the Global Challenge*, Gland and Cambridge: IUCN.

Marx, K. and Engels, F., (1971). *The Communist Manifesto*, New York: International Publishers.

McLean, G.N. (1996). Vocational and Technical Education and Training at Kenyatta University, Nairobi, Kenya (Project No. 75). St. Paul: Human Resource Development Research Center, University of Minnesota.

Myrstad, G. (1999). What can trade unions do to combat child labour? *Childhood*, 6, 75-88.

Pervez A.S., and Hussain K.S., (2005). *Access and Equity in Basic Education.* AEPAM Research Study No. 188; Academy of Educational Planning and Management: Islamabad.

Weiner, M., and Noman, O. (1995). *The Child and the State in India and Pakistan*, Karachi: Oxford University press.

Woodhead, M. (1999). Combating Child Labour: *Childhood.* 6, 27-49

Social Surveys of the Federal Bureau of Statistics, Government of Pakistan (http://www.statpak.gov.pk)

6

Sustainable Education and the Global Politics

Dharmarakshit Gautam

Education has always been critical for the development, and an indicator to mark the differentiation between the States. Recently in the name of placing it as a tool for the sustainable development, it has been utilized as a measure to establish hegemony by the developed State(s) over the developing ones. They are making the issue of sustainable development as they are facing the resource crunch and are blaming the latter for being inefficient (in resource utilization). Therefore, education is treated as an entity that may rescue these from their economic saturation or decline as may provide them access to exploit the market of the developing world in the name of spreading liberalization. The politics is to hold their present supremacy in the global affairs.

It has been aptly mentioned by Aristotle more than two thousand years before that "education is an ornament in prosperity and a refuge in adversity". At that point of time he might have realized the immense potential education was holding for an individual's development and so becomes inevitably crucial for a State's growth. This has had proved inarguably correct if we analyze the historical developments that took place in different States of the world before categorizing them into developed or developing. The vitality of education in the present age is well recognized by the United Nations, a body determined to have development of the entire world community. Recently education is understood as key factor for human growth and therefore included as the dynamic component in the human development index to estimate the real growth a State has made on annual basis. It would neither be wrong nor an exaggeration to say that the present development in the modern World could be attributed to education. Meanwhile it is noteworthy that there has been rapid and uneven development in different parts of the human habitations which did placed a question of everlasting survival due to limited carrying capacity of the nature we are bestowed with. Such a scenario made us to think more sensibly towards our future generations and thus came the concept of 'sustainable growth or development'.

In crude terms, sustainable development is a pattern of resource use that aims to meet human need while preserving the environment so that these needs can be met not only in the present but also for future generations. The best definition for it is given by the Brundtland Commission which says that "it is the development that meets the needs of the present without compromising the ability of the future generations to meet their own needs". The implication is clear that the development perspective(s) that hitherto had existed was not meant for uniform development of all, rather it was for strengthening the existing stratifications among the individuals and between the States at large. Now in the wake of limited carrying capacity of the nature, the existence is on stake, and therefore this *hullabaloo* about the sustainable development.

It is quite remarkable that United Nations conference on environment and development held at Rio de Janeiro in 1992 had influential role in linking the challenge of sustainability to education, and learning. In this, Agenda 21 emerged which identified education as critical for promoting sustainable development, improving the capacity of people to address environmental and developmental issues. More than a decade elapsed when the criticality of education for everlasting survival was recognized and from the year 2005 to 2014 was declared a decade of education for sustainable development by the United Nations. The credit for such development goes to United Nations Educational, Scientific and Cultural Organization (UNESCO) which place the argument that:

> "Universities must function as places of research and learning for sustainable development... Higher education should also provide leadership by practicing what they teach through sustainable purchasing, investments and facilities that are integrated with teaching and learning.... Higher education should emphasize experiential, inquiry based, problem solving, interdisciplinary systems approach and critical thinking. Curricula need to be developed including content, materials, and tools such as case studies and identification of best practices (UNESCO, 2004)".

In its world summit held in 2005, United Nations has identified three pillars of sustainable development, i.e. (a) Economic, (b) Social, and

(c) Environmental development. To this later Cultural development was appended. As mentioned earlier, Agenda 21 has emerged as vital input for such a process. It states broad public participation in decision making is fundamental prerequisite for achieving sustainable development. And the participation could be useful and functional only when people are made aware of complex relationship between scarce natural resources and growing human demand. Education has therefore important role to play in altering the process of depletion of human existence from the Earth.

The important riddle here is the fact that education is all encapsulating and therefore not devoid of ambiguity. Issues that are creating turbulence among the intellectuals around the globe is about the characteristics of education to be dispensed with, would it be modern or traditional, to whom it may be designated, and by whom it may be designed. It is an irrefutable fact that in the course of development, all societies of the world are geopolitically different and therefore are at different pedestal in terms of the global power they are holding. A more comprehensive analysis of the whole issue makes the issue of global politics more apparent in it. Several elements of the problem and also those which are posed as panacea for it do have tendency reflecting another process to establish hegemony in the world with the aid of the scientific and other advancements made by the present developed nations.

The question arises what kind of knowledge will best illuminate and equip to deal with issues of sustainability? The predicament is about which (disciplinary) knowledge may help in transcending towards sustainable future. Does it have supremacy of economic growth which is anthropocentric by default and has contradictions with the sustainable future of the world? Such an approach may satisfy the requirement posed by western knowledge which is more (economically) rational however the cultural (oriental) values might get sacrificed in this way and therefore could not be considered as coherent. Looking this way may imply that sustainable development is synonymous with material growth, maximization of profit and capital accumulation. It could be rightly mentioned here that history is a witness that import of one culture over the other on didactic terms might lead to failure of the one who does it. According to Michael Oakeshott (1962), "that attempts to simply import the principles and formal procedures of one culture into another are doomed to failure". It could be of great worth to mention the notion of 'cultural habitus' which education might buttress to keep its survival. It is viewed by the Bowers (1993) that education system in the west is based on rational traditions of 17th and 18th century thinkers as Descartes, Locke and Cassier. This made education their prisoner of cultural patterns of individualism, rational thinking and a dualistic view that distances man from nature. It is interesting to note that we still frame the ecological crisis as rationalistic and measurable problem. Therefore awareness and value to our own habitus may provide a solution for sustainable development.

To start with the concept of 'sustainable development' itself is beyond definitive comprehension as it is too vague and may imply differently for stratified horizon of the existing world order. The definition for sustainable development given by Brundtland Commission is having ample scope to turn it as open ended making it viable for the developed western world to impose its technocratic approach. While human action and political will are understood as crucial for sustainable development, its limits are not prescribed or left for the technological tools to determine.

Ideally the concept of sustainable development needs to be a collective endeavor without any supremacy of the west. However, the manner with which the concept is conceived and framed it is visible as if it is derived as a standard explanation of the west which is diplomatically imposed over other less powerful nations of the world. Meanwhile, the importance that local elements and cultural trait should have derived is elusive, giving way for dictatorial sway.

The culture of utilizing the available natural resources may be different for those who are having it bountifully but are unable to make big (returns) out it as the scientific advancements to utilize it efficiently has been developed somewhere else which are now the decision maker of everything. And now the repercussion of their striving for excellence has been borne by the former. Education for sustainable development was first described by chapter 36 of Agenda 21. It identified four major threats:

(a) Improve basic education.
(b) Reorient existing education to address sustainable development.
(c) Develop public understanding, awareness.
(d) Training.

It is pertinent to mention here that every challenge identified above is an additional responsibility for the developing countries as it may necessitate the requirement of revenue for these tasks. Also, if we try to diagnose the issue of sustainable development and fitting of education as a mechanism for its achievement we'd get a picture that holds political elements with economic ends. On the other hand, it may act as an opportunity to be a leader to govern the content (curricula) of such education (in the name of efficiency), and also to lend (financial) support which would be another way to get reward. One of the crucial and mandatory aspect of the sustainable education for everlasting development is its curriculum and the struggle for supremacy among nations for the same is ongoing and do have vested political as well as economic interests.

Curriculum of what is to be taught is a matter of great political significance as may act as tool to achieve the desired end of establishing the hegemony or maintaining the status quo. In the modern times (since we are aware about the international order) there has been paradigmatic shift in the operation of global politics. Previously the nature of global/ world politics was understood through the lenses of Realism or (later) Structural Realism which made security regime as prominent one to establish the supremacy. With the gradual development at several pockets of the world in the late twentieth century, this was shifted to pluralistic approach comprehensible through a more elaborate Complex Interdependence Theory. This novel approach became inevitable due to emergence of several democracies at the international horizon. Aspect of political regime could not be one (security) now rather it has to consider several of those and need to prioritize in accordance to the benefit it would be deriving in the presence of multilateral actors with varied importance. Such an opinion could be well described by the theory of complex interdependence, as the international politics ceased to be determined through uni-variate means (approach) and would rather demand multi-sectoral developments taking place simultaneously. Structural realism as stated by K. Waltz assumes military (power) as the sole aim of a State as it is fungible and could therefore overtake other issue areas. However, complex interdependence theory (by Robert Keohane and Joseph Nye) seeks to explain the dynamism involved in the present day world politics which requires several issue areas to be prioritized in the wake of multi polar world. In this scenario, military power could not be the supreme issue area.

Explanatory power of this theory has advanced over the realist and structural realist approach, but interestingly it may be noted that it failed to transcend the notion of supremacy among the hitherto existing powerful nations. Undoubtedly the nature of the politics underwent change but revised to reiterate aspiration to hold the power by the State. There is no denial to the fact that interdependence has become more explicit with the technological advancements while it is also true that it had ever existed since time immemorial. There has had always been some core and related periphery where core derived the maximum advantage in the name of holding efficient version of knowledge (to exploit the resources). It could be better understood if we see why the resource rich countries are still poor while the resource processing one are deriving benefit and had held their sway. Significantly this core periphery approach has not altered much and with the every new advancement at the global level it comes in a new avatar form.

Politics among different nations (with now more dynamic components) do have changed the core periphery linkage by taking it to a newer level in the predicament for mutual survival. The proponents of sustainable development hold the view that it may be possible if we have liberalized economies in the world an eminent aid for the ailing human survival. With a critical analysis Castros'[1] is juxtaposing the opinion which suggests for liberalized economies to undo poverty that may aid sustainable development. Such an approach is having contradictions as it may not alter the existing core periphery status. This would imply that balance of power won't change.

It is well placed that 'technology transfer' is instrumental to contribute for sustainable development. And such an endeavor is not free from cost which peripheral nations have to pay to the core nations with the export of their natural resources to the latter that in turn may lead inequalities. There is supportive argument for Capitalism and liberalism to have sustainable development. Environmental economists believe that capitalism may be sustainable as it tends to be technologically optimistic and therefore optimal utilization of the available natural resources. The author noting down the historicity of sustainable development points out several strands of opinion. One such opinion is that such a movement grew out as radical opposition to growth leading to ecological degradation (Pearce & Warford, 1993; Portney, 1992)[2], while Hays (1969)[3] saw it as a form of business utilitarianism. It is further claimed by the author that view of the World Bank is to promote capitalist trend and make it per se lasting.

World Bank suggests that capitalism would undo poverty, and provide technical awareness about the environment. Also, it would encourage property rights which may check the over exploitation of natural environment. This is a more diplomatic way to alter market situations of the States in favour of capitalism. It is noteworthy that such an approach ignores the issue of empowerment of periphery and takes it as dependent on developed core. There seem to have no regard for cultural and institutional diversity. Further, the model 'west' suggested is to have education for sustainable development is that of corporate mechanism for sustainable economic growth. This actually has contradictions with the ecological confrontations.

The curriculum and practices that has been adopted in the 'western' schools finds congruence with that of corporate sector seeking for profit making and resource exploitation. In the process, values that may be moral, personal, societal or environmental are lost. The saddest part is such neo-liberal business oriented education may be good for wealth accumulation but may part a difference from real value of 'good' that can't be judged through destructive economic rationality that valued efficiency and economic abstractions above people and community (Lynd, 1982)[4].

It is worthwhile to note down that such an approach is also inimical to the existing diversity of the bounteous nature. Undoubtedly, the economic growth approach is having its horns locked with the issue of ecological survival. It is no less than a diplomatic approach of the west to have doubly attitude. On the one hand it tries to create a hullabaloo about environmental degradation and therefore for sustainable development while keeping its other face shadowed under the neo-liberal approach. The witness is the curriculum and educational practice being professed in American schools is very much linked to the corporate world (Manteaw, 2010). This leaves the goal of our common future as precarious as it had been since its inception in the post modern times.

Critical approach presented by the environmental Marxists is relevant. It accurately places its argument that the present opinion about sustainable growth deemed to be primarily economic. Capitalist model of economic growth is diametrically opposite for the sustainable environment or nature. The very basic premise of the capitalist growth is the utmost exploitation of available natural resources and social capital, avoidance of wealth redistribution (or equity) both at the national and international level. This may lead towards unsustainable development.[5]

In the view of the ambiguity enshrined in the concept of sustainable development or for that matter education (as suggested in the frame) to achieve such an important goal becomes the discussion on the approaches holding dissent to the western or capitalist oriented suggestion for it. Environmental Marxists have criticized the very basic premise of capitalism as (exploitation) which may not yield equitable and henceforth the sustainable outcome. Marx believes that knowledge constructed under capitalism could not provide an effective solution for ecological degradation. This is because such a philosophy is based on material benefits or economic utilitarianism.

Among the various contradictions which Marxism exposes for capitalism, one relating to ecological decline needs attention here. It was made by O' Connor (1996)[6] who said capitalism has a contradiction between the production relations and the conditions of production. It is mentioned that conditions of production owe to 'external physical conditions', labour power (including training and degree of socialization), and the communal conditions (includes space and social environment). From this, it becomes clear that capital does not produce the condition of production but it's produced by nature and society. Rather capital while utilizing destroys the conditions of production. In pursuit of attaining more of surplus value a capitalist generally ignores the ecological and human aspect related to it making it (capitalism) functional. Therefore the result is decline of environment and the social process involved in it at subservient level. In the course of development process, capitalists have commodified the environment having devastating consequences for the developing world, who in the name of imitating the industrialization have added to ecological decline.

Apart from Marxists, Post Structuralists did place their critique of the present development. Their major concern is for uneven growth and related development between the developed (western) world and developing societies at large. The position of the latter is that of object for development where benefits are reaped by the former. The development model (of the western capitalists) was criticized by the post structuralists who with justification through question of 'ends' and 'means' makes it clear that development theorists would create their own discourse about (development) and transform system to suit its purpose.

Here comes the issue of cultural difference (or dissent) along with the relationship of core and periphery. Post Structuralists like Ferguson (1990)[7] holds opinion that how various structures as 'World Bank' operates for 'knowledge creation' that may serve the interests of the global power(s). Further, Escobar (another scholar) criticizing the capitalist model of development says that it creates a discourse where in the name of sustainable development the introduction of capitalism in the peripheral boundaries is channelized. It represents a dominance of culture of modernity[8].

Traversing in this manner there is every likelihood to have a top down, ethnocentric and technocratic approach, thus proving the cultural superiority of the west which focuses on the rational to create capitalism. And also (supposedly) hold the copyright to suggest the best direction leading for the (economically) sustainable development, as history has witnessed the cultural interpretation of development and underdevelopment.

In this sense, one crucial element of 'culture' comes into prominence in our discussion. Culture has had remained endemic to a particular geographical area and varies with that of other areas. The intense industry driven globalization has altered the notion by transcending the geographical as well as cultural boundaries. There seems to be no harm in the assimilation or confluence of the cultures in such a process. However, the utilitarian approach driving this phenomenon has made negative externalities to operationalize. It is witnessed that like other processes of development, new phenomenon of 'sustainable development' in the developing countries are made to borrow from the so called developed regions of the world thereby creating a new form of dependencies in the developing world with a supremacy of the western culture. One of the primary concerns here should be if there is need to emulate the western world by other developing pockets? And whether such trend may lead for sustainable development or would create a new dynamics to accelerate environmental degradation (Nurse, 2003)[9].

The area of exploitation (by the west) has broadened with the inclusion of education as tradable commodity. Liberalized education is suggested as one of the measure to ensure sustainable development. And when education is included in the list with other commercial activities (in GATS, General Agreement on Trade in Services), it's looked as a covetous opportunity to ameliorate the fiscal scenario of the west. It may be noted down that how education is viewed under GATS by the WTO? In the norms of WTO it is clearly mentioned that GATS excludes all the services provided solely by the government without any commercial purpose. And majority of the nations of the world are holding education on mixed basis. Therefore, with a very bleak margin of distinction, education has majorly included in GATS and under WTO norms there is allowance to other member countries to invade.

Those who are propounding for sustainable development as need of the hour are actually suggesting for privatization and opening of the entire world economy making every State available for exploitation. These States are making opinion to have a new frame of curriculum with primacy of certain disciplines that may require import of aid from these developed communities. It did undermine the locally available culture and knowledge of a developing State. Looking back for almost five decades we could see the concept of sustainable development was well conceived in commission for university education under Dr. Radhakrishnan (1948) where it is written that "the most important and urgent reforms needed in education is to transform it, to endeavor to relate it to life, needs and aspirations of the people, and thereby make it a powerful instrument of social, economic, and cultural transformation necessary for the realization of the national goals. For this purpose, education should be developed so as to increase productivity, achieve social and national integration, accelerate the process of modernization, and cultivate social, moral, and spiritual values"[10].

Therefore, education is meant to understand the diversity still striving to be self sufficient utilizing the minimum. And the education that has been promoted in the name of development by the capitalist countries is actually having a paradox with the sustainable development. Such education has the tendency to increase the habit to consume goods which increases the threat to sustainability as consumption drives the resource extraction for manufacturing the consumable goods and related services.

There is no denial to the fact that there has been erratic development among human societies around the world posing a great challenge for nature to retrieve back to normal. And further education does have a critical role to keep the limits maintained. However, important aspect to be dealt here is who will have supremacy over others in such a framework. Whose interests (to develop) would be kept at bay in the name of maintaining the ecology? Till the time global politics has had existed where few or one (powerful) State(s) have kept their economy and development on all other(s). With the gradual elapse of time, such development made ecological confrontation and also simultaneous economic stagnation which may ultimately lead to doing away with the supremacy. In an attempt to avert this, global powers have developed the concept of 'sustainable development' which is oxymoron, and is only a means to achieve their desired ends. The need is to shift the focus where global powers are not central and thus equal participation of the developing world in designing such future is made essential.

NOTES

1. For details see Castro, J. Carlos (2004) Sustainable Development: Mainstream and Critical Perspectives, *Organisation Environment,* 17; 195 doi: 10.1177/1086026604264910, http://oae.sagepub.com/cgi/content/abstract./17/2/195.
2. *Ibid.*
3. *Ibid.*
4. Lynd, S. (1982) Fight Against Shutdowns, Singlejack Books, San Pedro, CA, as cited in Manteaw (2010).

5. Cited at 'Sustainable Development: A Review of International Literature', Scottish Executive Social Research, 2006. Also, available at www.scotland.gov.uk/social research.
6. As cited in Castro (2004).
7. Cited in Castro (2004).
8. Cited in Castro (2004).
9. Nurse, Keith (2003) Development: Unthinking the Past, NACLA Journal, 37.3, as cited in Nurse, Keith (2006) Culture as the fourth pillar of Sustainable Development, Commonwealth Secretarial, London.
10. Cited in 'Role of Higher Education and Sustainable Development in India' by Dr. Nidhi Sharma, Preeti Verma, and Praveen Kumar. The article is available at http://cbsmohali.org/wp-content/downloads/n4e6850c1437d7. pdf

REFERENCES

Bonnet, Michael (1999). Education for Sustainable Development: A Coherent Philosophy for Environmental Education?, *Cambridge Journal of Education*, Vol. 29, No. 3, pp. 313-324.

Bossel, Hartmut (1999). Indicators for Sustainable Development: Theory, Method, Applications—A Report to the Balaton Group, International Institute for Sustainable Development, Canada.

Castro, J. Carlos (2004). Sustainable Development: Mainstream and Critical Perspectives, Organization and Environment, Vol. 17, 195, http://oae.sagepub.com/cgi/content/abstract/17/2/195.

Jones, Paula, Selby, David and Sterling, Stephen (ed.) (2010). Sustainability Education—Perspectives and Practice Across Higher Education, Earthscan, London, U.K.

Isiksal, Huseyin (2004). To What Extend Complex Interdependence Theorists Challenge to Structural Realist School of International Relations?, *alternatives*, Vol. 3, No. 2 & 3, pp. 130-156.

Manteaw, Offeibob (2010). Education in Global Environment Politics: Why the Discourse of Education for Sustainable Development Needs Attention, *International Journal of Environment and Sustainable Development*, Vol. 9, Nos. 1/2/3, pp. 74-90.

Newell, Peter (2000). Globalization and the New Politics of Sustainable Development, In Bendell, Jem (ed.) (2000). *Terms for Endearment: Business, NGOs and Sustainable Development*, Greenleaf Publishing, Sheffield, U.K.

Nurse, Keith (2006). Culture as the Fourth Pillar of Sustainable Development, Commonwealth Secretarial, London.

Tilburg, Dabiella, Stevenson, B. Robert, Fien, John, Schreuder, Danie (2002). Education and Sustainability Responding to the Global Challenge, IUCN.

Waltz, N. Kenneth (2000). Structural Realism After the Cold War, *International Security*, Vol. 25 (1), pp. 5-41.

7

Rethinking Sustainable Development

Inclusion of Social Dimensions to Sustainability

Sreekala Edannur

The understanding of the meaning and structure of the term Sustainable Development requires an exploration into its semantic roots. Literally sustainable development means sustaining something or continuing something. The term is inconsistently interpreted either as sustaining growth or as a form of societal change that, in addition to traditional development objectives, has the objective or constraint of ecological sustainability (Lele, 1991). A basic understanding of what the term means is required before any further thinking on sustainable development. Lele's framework of sustainable development provides a basic understanding of the meaning of the word 'sustainability'. What is intended of sustainability—what does it literally mean, does it connote an ecological sense, and does it connote a social sense is to be made clear for establishing a conceptual framework for the term. The literal meaning refers to the continuation of anything. The ecological meaning relates to maintaining the 'ecological basis of human life' within a time-based structure, indicating concern for both the future and the present. In describing the social meaning of Sustainable Development, Lele (1991) uses Barbier's (1987) notion of social meaning, which focuses on maintaining desired 'social values, institutions, and culture. This also sounds similar to the theories of consensus theorists of society which call for basic agreement to values, institutions and culture in a society for human progress. In the forgoing section is a figure to provide an interpretative understanding of the term sustainable development. The figure and the following discussion is meant to fill the gap in the literature on Sustainable Development. The discussion emphasizes the importance of socio cultural dimensions of sustainable development.

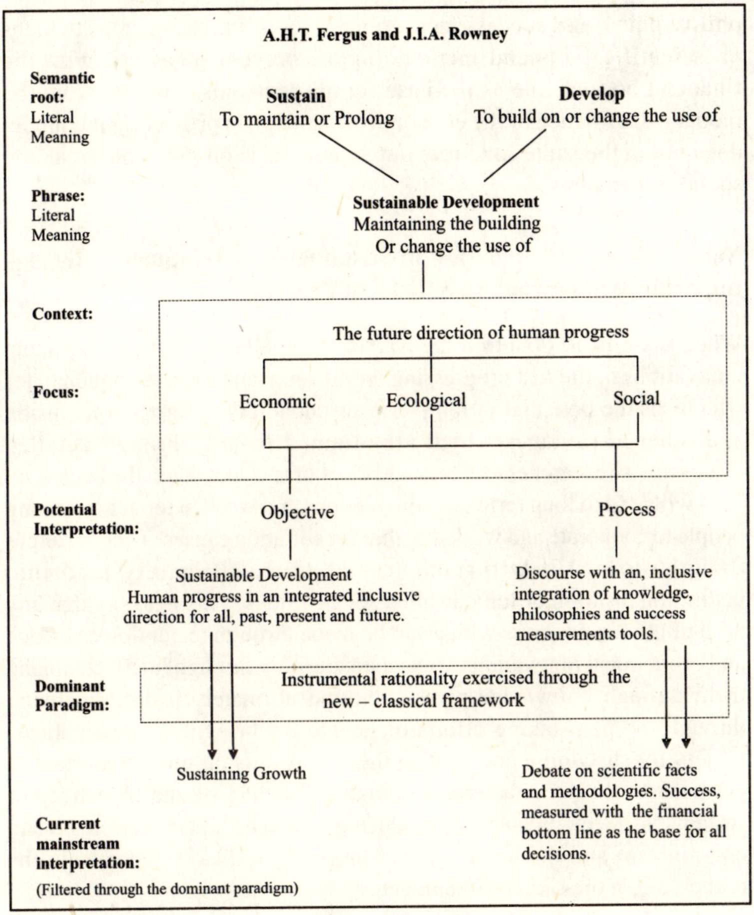

Fig. 7.1: Semantic Framework of Sustainable Development

The terms sustain in the model means maintaining and to construct on what is existing and also changing the uses of existing. When this meaning is placed in the context it shows the entire mechanism of human progress in terms of its objectives and the processing. The model projects the dominant paradigm of sustainable development as decided both by its objectives and process and very clearly depicts the prominence of neo classical economic framework for human progress to be effective. The process dimension is projected as a very important dimension of any kind of sustaining development that is an emphasis on discourses with an inclusive integration of knowledge, philosophies, and success measurement tools which includes debates on scientific facts and methodologies, success measures with the financial bottom-line as the base for all decisions. Though from the model a dominance of the economic dimension is projecting the model does not at the same time rule out an emphasis on the ecological and social dimensions.

Nature of Social Dimension in Sustainable Development Model—Importance of Discourses in Human Progress

When there is no doubt on the role of reforms and swift and big bang innovations in the fast progressing world, slow and incremental changes which has the potential of long term sustainability in terms of inclusion and other advantages which are attained mostly through detailed discussions, researches, debates and discourses have taken the back seat. This will lead to long term erosion of ethics and weaken tendency among people to cooperate and work together for common causes. These changes though slow still withstand test of time, ultimately lead into institutionalisation of long awaited social values. This is to say that any kind of human progress which can be made through technology, science and economical innovations are sustainable only through intellectualising them through knowledge production and ultimately institutionalising through the painstaking efforts of people for bringing changes in the society for sustaining and sharing them. It is thus far more important to get back to the process with a thorough standing on the objectives of sustainable development since producing cannot be separated from certain environment and the quality of the by-product always depends on the processing in the right environment.

The Contradictions

The understanding of sustainable development is not without problems. The major weakness of the sustainability literature is the failure of intellectual traditions to link nature with social and economic realities. The potential strengths and weaknesses of Marxist approaches to the environment, which view the environment as a commodity under capitalism, are linked to the production of nature via biotechnology and genetic engineering. The weakness of Marxist theory in failing to integrate reproduction and ecological sustainability in its account of the developmental process is paralleled by the failure in the reproductive and biotechnological sciences to address the social and economical implications of transforming nature (Redclift, 1987). Likewise chances for a conclusive model for sustainable development is limited by the efforts of intellectuals to separate the social and natural sciences. For these same reasons it is also not possible to conclude on an effective model for sustainable development. The founding fathers of sociology, Weber, Comte and Durkheim struggled for establishing a synchronic view of development. Synthesizing social processing with natural processing was seen problematic by these sociologists.

Social Description of Sustainability

Max Weber observed that 'the belief in the value of scientific truth is not derived from nature but is a product of definite cultures'. Merton (1957) adds to this, 'The persistent development of science occurs only in societies of a certain order, subject to a peculiar complex of tacit presuppositions and institutional constraints. The continuity of science requires the active participation of interested and capable persons in scientific pursuits. This support of science is assured only by appropriate cultural conditions. It is, then, important to examine those controls which motivate scientific careers which select and give prestige to certain scientific discipline sand blur others. It will become evident that changes in institutional structure may curtail, modify or possibly prevent the pursuit of science. This is cited here to highlight importance of prevailing culture in a society, maintenance of a certain social structure and also modifications and changes in the social structure for any human progress to be sustained. According to Weber it is the individual, who contributes to social action, and for Marx it is social action which transforms the world, but for Durkheim it is the collective action of people that transforms the world. Though contradictions exist, maintenance of a social structure and modifications—could be transformative—is the touchstone of any kind of development and sustenance. As the model above shows, Sustainable Development as a process, growth and change is required and when referring to an objective means satisfying basic needs. This is the concept of social inclusion which makes the sustaining development a contradictory concept. But this contradiction makes the concept more meaningful. As a society, our goals should be looking at development that sustains values, reflecting progress in our relationships with one another as human beings, our place in the natural environment, and consequently developments in what it means to be human (Stead and Stead, 2000).

Whit ford, Wong K. (2009) conducted a study which offers a rich quantitative analysis of the political and social foundations of environmental sustainability using broad measures of sustainability in a variety of development and geographic contexts. This study offers a fill in the gaps in the sustainability literature. The results found Democracy receiving a moderate supporting the measurements of sustainability. The study also found varying patterns of relationships between the measurements of sustainability and social foundations for sustainability, including the effect of economic development (both current and historical), business practices, the presence of religious affiliations, and demographic factors. Together, these findings portray a complex and varied set of foundations for environmental sustainability.

Criticisms of the Interpretations of Sustainable Development

There is a clear and wide gap in terms of conceptual clarity of the term Sustainable Development though it is difficult due to the contradictions the term carry with it. The combining of economic, social and ecological dimensions in development requires painstaking efforts to synthesise. Lele, S.M. (1991) criticizes the view of Sustainable Development for its failure to develop a solid conceptual foundation that would produce clearly defined criteria and policies. Four broad weaknesses contributed to this failure (Lele, 1991):

Lele identifies several weaknesses with the main stream definitions of Sustainable Development and its current interpretations:

1. *A simplistic characterization of the problems of poverty and environmental degradation.* Lele challenges the assumption that poverty causes environmental degradation and that economic growth is necessary for environmental sustainability.
2. *Ambiguously conceptualized central objectives of the paradigm:* development, sustainability and participation. Distinctions between the goals and means of attaining sustainable development are ambiguous. Lele also questions the neo-classical economic assumptions that (a) economic growth necessarily constitutes development; and (b) economic growth reduces poverty. Distinctions should be made between ecological and social sustainability, such that the dynamic interplay between social structures and environmental conditions are recognized. Finally, Lele challenges the notions that (a) 'participation' can

be equated with justice and equity and that (b) participation necessarily yields ecologically sustainable practices.

3. *Inadequate action strategies adopted in the face of incomplete knowledge and ambiguity.* Lele argues that many 'sustainable development' policies have not recognized (a) the inequities of the global monetary exchange system and that (b) 'free trade' has different impacts in differing economic systems and it does not necessarily yield equitable, sustainable development. Consequently, policy prescriptions in terms of international trade and economic relations, sustainable agriculture and tropical forests are inconsistent and inadequate.

As in the Rowney model, the social dimensions of Sustainable Development which is objective oriented will gradually give its way to one of process domination where in big bang innovations started taking over. And the concept may weaken further by its objectives and become a supplement to the dominant paradigm of economic growth. So there is a larger fundamental separation between the social dimensions and thinking based on the rational logic of the ecologic—economical paradigm. The ecologic—economical paradigm, manifested through the cognitive structure of the economic framework, moved the meaning of Sustainable Development from an inclusive exploration of objectives to an instrumental debate about process, a process in which the measure of success was economic, allowing no room for alternative measurement criteria (Lawson, 1997).

Sustainability as a Social Process

Sustainability is deeply a socio-cultural subject matter, not just an ecological matter. Nature is defined by the social processes which shape a society's interactions and relationships. Then the matter is: how can societies regulate and change their social processes and structures so as to ensure the chances for development of future generations? Sebastian Brandl defines sustainability as the relationship between the social and ecological systems, which needs to be shaped in such a way that it will not destabilise the system as a whole: Environmental sustainability turns out to be closely linked to supposedly internal problems of social structure, such as social justice, gender equality and political participation Griebler *et al.* (2005). In this sense, sustainability describes a topic of research that is basically social, addressing virtually the entire 'process by which societies manage the material conditions of their reproduction, including the social, economic, political and cultural principles that guide the distribution of environmental resources (Becker *et al.*, 1999).

Society and Nature

Sustainable development should allow the satisfaction of existing needs in the long term, which means that sustainability ought to be directed towards the relationships between nature and society. These relationships should not just be functional for a short period of time but also make it possible for future generations to meet their needs. Based on the concept of needs 'sustainability' is a genuinely anthropocentric term.

A major driving force behind society and societisation seems to be—in the broadest sense—the creation of opportunities to meet one's needs (Malinowski, 1944). For that purpose, societies have come up with a number of different functional systems and institutions. Among them, economy, politics and culture have come to play a special role in the sustainability discourse, even though this may not be reasonable from a systematic point of view. These three interdependent functional systems and their particular institutions, which can only be separated from each other at an analytical level, are essential for shaping and controlling the relationships between society and nature. Social coherence within societies, which is both their condition and outcome, is vital for the creation and working of these systems. With regard to content, these three systems are mainly differentiated by their functionality (Parsons, 1966):

- Economy includes all services, institutions and infrastructures in the agricultural, industrial and service sectors that are used for (material) reproduction. Economy as a functional system consists of formal, monetary and informal economic activities as well as the consumption of the produced goods and services.
- The functional system of politics comprises the formation of political attitudes, Opinions, orientations and decisions as well as the implementation thereof by means of specific activities, measures and institutions.
- The cultural system includes all cultural practices and interpretation patterns of a society, which find expression in lifestyles and life forms, social orders and the legitimacy thereof (e.g., gender order, dealing with otherness), moral concepts, religion, etc. The cultural practices and interpretation patterns inherent to different societies are highly divergent and subject

to change over time. They represent the framework within which economic and political processes are formed and legitimized.

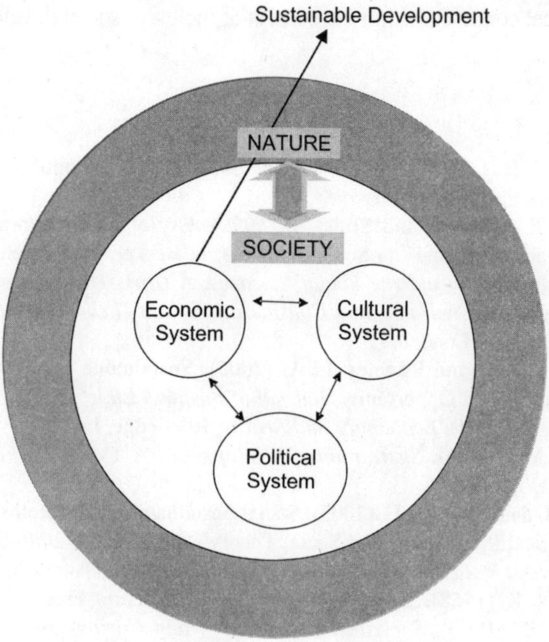

Fig. 7.2: Schematic Portrayal of Sustainable Development and the Relationships Between Society and Nature

Final Reflections

Academicians and other members of society should come together to develop ideas that integrate the environment, society and polity. Such integration would encourage discourses that are discussed in this chapter for promoting the advancement of society based on a inclusive whole, focusing on the present and caring the future generations. Ideas on social sustainability should open up space for interdisciplinary studies for development. Academicians in other fields are far more suspicious of economists since like Marx, economists will eventually reduce everything to what they can measure or set a price on, and for this reason many social scientists are reticent about collaborating in such combining efforts which will be a practical step towards solving problems related to sustainability. Enriching the theoretical context within which the social variables are embedded should be the concern of academia of all disciplines. Working closely with academia in varied disciplines from where concepts are drawn can minimize the dangers of meaningless and short term changes. Finally, it is important to firmly embed all kinds of economic and ecological concerns within the context of inclusive social development.

REFERENCES

Barbier, E.B. (1987). The Concept of Sustainable Economic Development, *Environmental Conservation.*

Becker, E., Jahn, T. and Stiess, I. (1999). Exploring Uncommon Ground: Sustainability and the Social Sciences, in Becker, E. and Jahn, T. (Eds.): *Sustainability and the Social Sciences, A Cross-Disciplinary Approach Integrating Environmental Considerations into Theoretical Reorientation*, Zed Books, London.

Fergus, A.H.T. and Rowney J.I.A. (2005). Sustainable Development: Lost Meaning and Opportunity. *Journal of Business Ethic.*

Lawson, T. (1997). *Economics and Reality*. Routledge, London.

Lele, S.M. (1991). *Sustainable Development: A Critical Review*. World Development.

Littig, B. and Griebler, E. (2005). Social Sustainability: A Catchword between Political Pragmatism and Social Theory', *Int. J. Sustainable Development.*

Malinowski, B. (1944). *A Scientific Theory of Culture*, Chapel Hill.

Merton, R.K. (1968). *Social Theory and Social Structure.* Free Press, NewYork.

Parsons, T. (1966). *Societies, Evolutionary and Comparative Perspectives*, Englewood Cliffs, New Jersey.

Redclift, M.R. (1987). *Sustainable Development: Exploring the Contradictions.* Psychology Press.

Stead, J.H. and E. Stead (2000). Eco-Enterprise Strategy: Standing for Sustainability, *Journal of Business Ethics.*

Whitford, A.B. and Wong, K. (2009). Political and Social Foundations for Environmental Sustainability. *Political Research Quarterly.*

8

Science Education and Sustainable Development

M.N. Bapat

> 'Nothing has such power to broaden the mind as the ability to investigate systematically and truly all that comes under thy observation in life'. —*Marcus Aurelius*

If we go by Ralph Waldo Emerson, 'Men love to wonder, and that is the seed of science'. Humans essentially are entrepreneurs by nature. If it is so, the discoveries no wonder would follow. But according to Carl Sagan, 'science is a way of thinking much more than it is a body of knowledge'. This philosophy on pondering over and honest persuasion leads to science education.

In this fast growing science-technology culture, social changes are quite conspicuous. No aspect of human being are left untouched viz., desire for acquisition of knowledge; eagerness for know-how of devices (everyday new gadgets are pouring in) and how to use those for their own advantage; how life can be led safely, healthily and comfortably; how new skills could be inculcated; how scientific attitudes need to be developed; and always struggle for excelling to edge over contemporaries. To allow inquiring minds to take on activities for satiating their quest at a pace set by the learner herself/himself are the developmental activities. Once a learner takes up a task she/he will follow all steps of scientific method namely: conceptualize, hypothesis, design, experiment upon, analyze the data collected to find relationship and discuss with the colleagues for validity or otherwise. The results, however, need to be tested very seriously and cautiously. The feasible application of the outcome is development.

Essentials of Education for Sustainable Development, which must become part and parcel of teaching learning process, include the events that if allowed to happen will save humanity and environment from destruction. The concern and pre and post efforts for minimizing damage that a disasters causes, non-interference with the happenings of natures' own vagaries (climate changes, biodiversity, disturbing natures' mass distribution etc.). Here we may remember what George Bernard Shaw wanted to tell 'Science never solves a problem without creating ten more'.

Let us find out what made Einstein to say "*Generations to come will scarce believe that such a one as this ever in flesh and blood walked upon this earth.*" The determination of Gandhiji was of higher order. He used to take decision as per his conviction. When to pursue a matter till goals or achieved, when to agree for midway solution, when to support enemy, when to withdraw, when to become lenient, when to show power, when to take a stronger step, when to convince, how to lead sincere life, what action would be beneficial to a larger group, how to get first-hand experience of people of the country, on whom to depend, whose advice need to be considered, how to advocate for a cause, how to defend, how to minimise violence, how to protest without anger etc. The glaring examples are salt satyagrah, *chouri choura* episode, round table conference and alike. Neither succeeds an aggressive or idle. The proverb is two kinds of people fail in life—one: those who reflect for welfare but do not act; two: those who act without reflecting over.

Teaching-Learning *vis-à-vis* Sustainable Development

> 'The Prime Minister of India, at a meeting that I co-chaired a few months ago, stated that any development that is not sustainable is not development.' — Maurice Strong

Sustainable Development at the first instance requires participatory teaching and learning. It becomes a mandate for teachers and teacher-educators to devise methods that will motivate and empower learners to change and react positively on pupils' responses and take action to ensure measures that are appropriate for sustainable development. The attitude should be such which will promote pupils' competencies with respect to critical thinking, foresightedness of future scenarios (tackling challenges and problems) and making judicious decisions in a collaborative way.

The pioneers having done and exerting for sustaining development is the Global Development and Environment Institute (GDAE) is a Research Institute at Tufts University (USA). It, through research, policy work, projects, curriculum development, conferences and lot of other activities, they are doing spade work.

Education for Sustainable Development (ESD)

Groundwork or foundation for sustainability of education worldwide starts from literacy and developing skills. All activities end up with product suggesting lot of ideas for developing devices. The devices fabrication requires creativity, handicraft skill, broad thinking, foresightedness, test of viability, understanding complexities etc. To achieve those objectives Science Education becomes of foremost importance. Education causes changes in approach to a problem. It goes like-focusing at the problem, looking at it from different angles, analyzing methods available, find most suitable answers through asking various question for its validity (if necessary modified, cause and effect), search for hands with best skill, taking services of that skilled person, looking at the product critically, make/seek corrections (if need be), providing it to sample for standardizing-testing and finally putting it for use at a larger scale. At different stages advice from experts/critic always helps.

Knowing is not Enough

Various approaches to ESD are to encourage people to understand the complexities of, reasoning for, and consistencies in proposition. Let us see following examples to clarify points a) where could not pass on the knowledge; b) where superstitions dominated which disseminated very fast and c) where we are not sure whether instances can be right or wrong. Are all these against ESD?

Task: Classify following examples in to examples of concerns, proper examples for ESD, non-examples and examples that need serious discussion.

a. Rope making and its application in a variety of situations is not new. It is generally made from fibres whether it is coir, taken from plantain or corn stem, cotton, silk, animal skin/ hair,(obtained from glass/steel or different metals, nylon, spider or sisal etc.- may be a few exceptions), or any other. General understanding says when fibres are twined compactly; the friction between them is the cause of strength of the rope. If this were the sole reason, what is written in bracket is also not exception. But ancient scientist knew the reason which was not properly passed on and we had to wait till microscope was discovered. Many might have noticed long beautiful black hairs of young Indian women. When they comb it, it is from skull to end and not otherwise. Further, they are thick at roots and become thinner towards end. See below why it is so. For brevity it is shown straight.

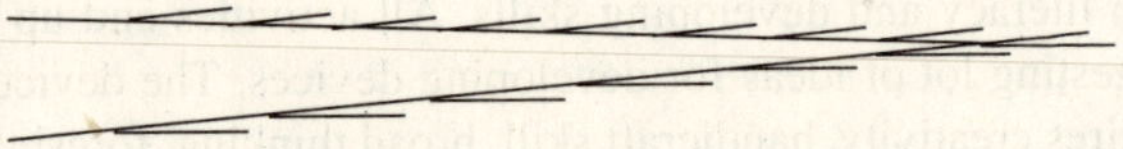

Now let them assemble

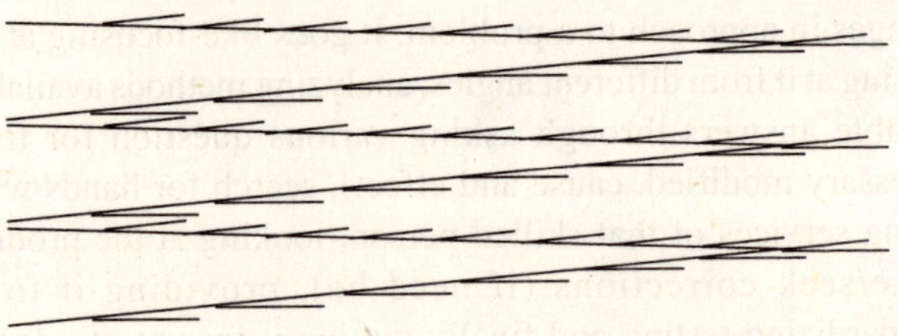

It can be observed that left side can hardly be compressed, whereas right side can be easily compressed. And hairs appear to thin towards end. If oily hairs are pulled from left to right, our hand will slip.

Now observe another combination where upper hair tapers towards right and another hair below tapers towards left. If brought closer its not only friction

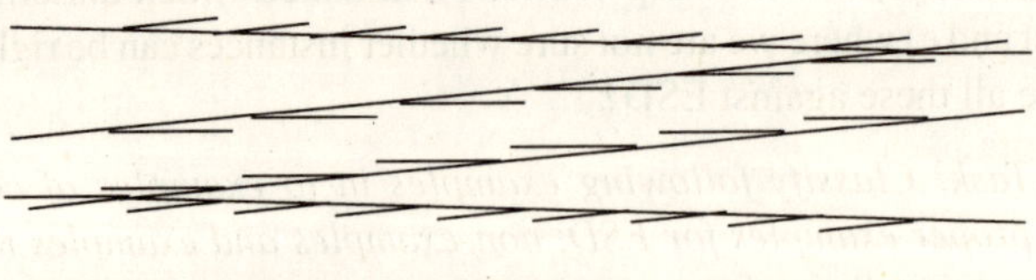

But locking of branches also happens. Lens was discovered by Bacon sometime in 1052. It tells passing on the knowledge to next is not enough, but providing the reason is also equally important. It took another 400 odd years to make use of lenses. This very character of sharing/discussing/interacting was probably missing. Due to small kingdoms and their rivalry made reasoning missing along with a good deal of information also.

b. Use of stick by persons climbing or moving on slippery/untidy path is age old phenomenon. The message that it helps in locating centre of gravity was missing.

c. Herbal medicines have a history of about 4000 years now. We may not expect it was one day's job. It might have taken hundreds of year's accumulated experience. Everything spoilt because of non-recording facility or writing on leaves/so called Tad Patras.

d. When a black cat comes towards you from front, your objective of doing something fails disparately. How to classify scientifically?

e. Alien land on earth with qualities unimaginable and go away with a speed unimaginable. Flying soccer is not newly coined word.

f. Black magic and act mesmerize, to what extent it can be relied upon?

g. Saints possess wonderful powers.

h. Shri Vinoba Bhave recalls (in his talks on Gita), one person comes to him to help him complete his '*Yagna*' by repeating a mantra some number of times to please the God. Vinobaji wondered whether God needs a definite number of chanting for *HIS* favour.

i. If a cock cries several times in front of your house. It is a bad omen. Cock does not touch *PIND* of dead if its invisible presence is there.

j. Deers' move haphazardly, birds become uneasy when calamity is in offing.

k. Think of devil and devil is here (sub-consciousness prevails).

l. A blessing from the bottom of the heart motivates.

m. Faith gives strength.

Some Special Features of Education for Sustainable Development

> 'Nothing has such power to broaden the mind as the ability to investigate systematically and truly all that comes under thy observation in life'. —*Marcus Aurelius*

To see that ESD happens, a few aspects need to be cautiously pursued. These are:

1. There is need to have cohesion and understanding among people at the helm in the interest of humanity. Ego should be out. The decisions and acting on it must have consensus through negotiation.
2. Values agreed upon must be meticulously observed.

3. Dialogue between those in power across the globe with participative cooperation.
4. Curriculum makers may be empowered to find out best ways of dissemination and preservation of knowledge. Not only in software, but also in physically safe custody, best is carving on the stones. Green Education Foundation is encouraging students to become green environmental stewards. United Nations is observing 2004-2014 as ESD decade and explores opportunity and vision for role of education in learning for awareness, training, interaction, maximum involvement in progressive efforts.

Thus we find that Education for Sustainable Development requires far-reaching changes in the way education is often practiced today.

What History Tells About Concerns for Educating People?

> "Gender equality is more than a goal in itself. It is a precondition for meeting the challenge of reducing poverty, promoting sustainable development and building good governance".
>
> — *Kofi Annan*

We do not have much access to age old history of mankind though presence different kinds of animals, plant kingdom are supposed to be there on earth. In Indian context, however, the state of development of ancient India is known, through substantial scribbles, and carvings on walls at different places are available. The entrepreneurs and different visitors from China and other countries have jotted down their experiences about India. Lot of literature was concentrated in two major universities and individual Gurukuls.

From the angle of science, philosophy and art, ancients knew about health and hygiene, different tricks of defenses and weapons of iron and stone, use of basic machines like wedge, pulley, wheels, levers; exploring techniques like diggers, ropes, sticks; food preparation devices like fire, copper utensils and earthen wares; different skills (64 in number) including painting, carvings on stone, making tidy living space, ornaments etc.

Research shows that education is key to sustainable development. From present day point of view sustainable development of a nation must work on following major themes. (History tells enmity and ignoring capability have adverse effect on development.)

1. Agricultural productivity commensurate with needs.

2. Reduction in population growth.
3. Preservation of environment from the point of extinction of animal and plant kingdom.
4. Respect and empower women.
5. Value literacy and knowledge of numerals
6. Adopt always time tested and newer technology.
7. Reduce difference in living standard between different groups of society, without harming environment and justice.

What We can Learn from Past Experiences?

> 'Bad times have a scientific value. These are occasions a good learner would not miss'. —*Ralph Waldo Emerson*

It is not differences but sharing and caring is essence of ESD. Individual's greed and power hungriness divided the earth (on sea and on surface) into countless kingdoms. The rulers hardly bothered about preserving heritage or knowledge. For development it is peace and harmony that is vital. UNO (1945) is striving for best possible harmony and dispensing with hegemony with conscious efforts. Earlier efforts, after First World war were almost failures.

The International Center for Leadership stressed in the conference that partnership is essential for ESD. The conference agreed upon the *Partnership's Vision—"sustainable development integrated into education and learning in the United States;"* and *Mission—to "leverage the UN Decade to foster education for sustainable development in the United States"* had a clearly spelled the need of partnership. The areas of partnership being formation of Action Teams: (Marketing, Outreach, Funding, ICT, Youth involvement etc.); Sector Teams: (K-12, Higher Education, Faith Communities, Business, and Communities.); Executive Teams and Volunteer Leadership were envisaged. Different teams were assigned different tasks.

The UN Decade and the U.S. Partnership provided international and national context for such efforts, helping to promote and strengthen education for sustainable development especially in the United States which had a leading role. Education is an essential tool for achieving sustainability. People around the world are afraid that current economic development trends are not sustainable and that public awareness, education, and training are key issues to make society moving towards sustainability. Beyond that, there is little agreement. People argue about the meaning of sustainable development and whether or not it is attainable.

They have different visions of what sustainable societies will look like and how they will function. These same people wonder why educators have not moved more quickly to develop education for sustainability programmes. The lack of agreement and definition has hindered the efforts to design education for sustainable development (ESD) forward.

What are the Obstacles in Sustaining Development?

> "A scientific truth does not triumph by convincing its opponents and making them see the light, but rather because its opponents eventually die and a new generation grows up that is familiar with it".
>
> —*Max Planck*

Let us recall what noted scientists said about electromagnetic equations which were put in proper shape by Maxwell. *"Mc Cullough in 1843 gave correct equations for the behaviour of light in crystals. But there is no real material whose mechanical properties could possibly satisfy those equations. Since light is oscillations that must vibrate in something—hence we cannot believe this abstract equation business".*

Clearly, scientist at those times did not accept abstract ideas. All ideas were to be supported with concrete examples. Thus it was taboo for inventor. She/he had to demonstrate what she/he wanted to tell.

The other constrain was unless you please the lords of the place, whatever is invented/discovered will not be approved. A patenting system in years to come may also become stumbling block if not justifiable.

Too much disparity among peoples of any nation has to have its bad implications. Water exploitation will also be a big barrier, if not handled in time.

Nations going nuclear may mar development and sustenance itself may pose problems of different kinds from health to survival.

Case Study on Synthetic Products

Positive and Negative Approach to Use of Poly Products: A Case Study

Before synthesis of polymer compounds and application at a small scale and then on large scale is being protested by environmentalist. We list down positive and negative points related to it. The reader will decide and review.

Background

The cooking material used by poor and villagers mud pots. Let us forget about quality. It being a bad conductor required large quantity of fuel. Water storing, food product storing was also done in large earthenware pots. This was so till 60 years ago. But the life and tendency to break was ***one*** and bacteria/undesirable material into pores was the ***second*** reason to avoid it. At this instance production and availability in large scale—*aluminium*—was a boon in disguise. Water fetching vessels and cooking utensils readily replaced earthenware. It was cheaper with better life span was its added advantage. When plastic products came in it replace everything except cooking vessels.

Merits and Demerits of Poly Products

Merits	*Demerits*
Cheap-cost friendly Easy to synthesize Easy to mould in desired shape Make device compact Good insulator Available in many compositions It is recyclable Poor friendly Its bags of thickness > 40 microns, can be reused if degradable It has degradable form also Its composites are finding use in dedicated devices. Hardened ones are used in doors and vehicles. So it is cost effective, saving metals and wood which are water resistant It is if reused can save one use paper bags	Thinner material is susceptible to break Non degradable Low quality takes on fire with obnoxious smoke Devices are less sturdy Aging makes is useless Discarded product disposition is difficult Seconds (recycled) has very less life span Once broken can hardly be mended Poly bags thinner than 40 microns are susceptible to harm animal life Non degradable poly products difficult to dispose If kept away from animals, its waste can be laid at base of tar roads which might increase life of the road. But if burnt, its smoke plays disaster role. If thrown discriminately, it chokes pipe lines and untidiness flourishes Say no to thinner poly bags, for safe environment, safe ozone layer

Will the reader 'Make a case for thermocol'?

How to Tackle the Problems?

> "People think of the inventor as a screwball, but no one ever asks the inventor what he thinks of other people."
>
> —*Charles Kettering*

In countries where many people live below poverty bench mark, poverty reduction must be a prominent place where much needs to be done. Exploiting nature, for accessible luxury has grown to un-pardoning dimensions. Excavation at Kolar Gold Fields (KGF Bangalore) has crossed danger level, coal extraction and other ores are also no exception. Petroleum may see its extinction soon. De-forestation has already gone beyond our control because of our lust for accruing unlawful wealth. In short we have deceived our future generations. This has happened only during last 100 years or so. Population growth and use of excessive toxicants have to be delimited and hence the aspect of sustainable consumption must be observed seriously. Let us pen down our problems and propose tentative solutions.

Envisioning: The premise is we know what exactly we want to do. We have to work out how to achieve the objective.

Critical reflection—learner learns best when she/he ruminate over problem attacks it with several related or even ridiculous question. Looking in to pros and cones help to recognize the assumptions and suitability of underlying knowledge, perspective and opinions. Critical thinking skills help to learn how to examine different causes for sustainable development. How to do justice to sustainable development? Educate the society by acting according to following scheme.

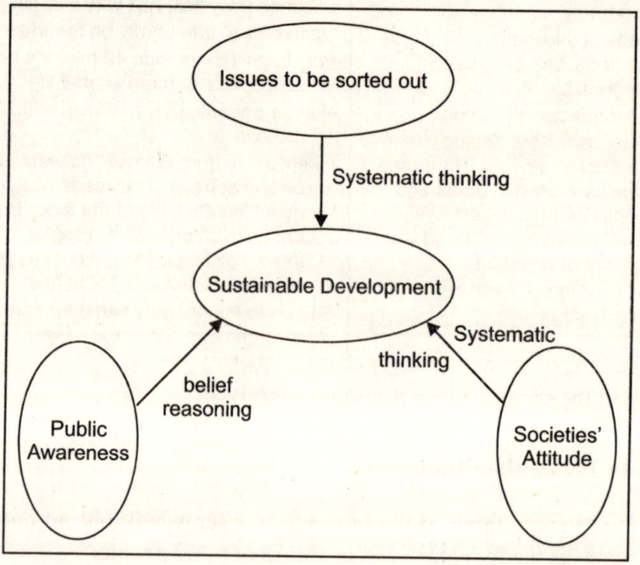

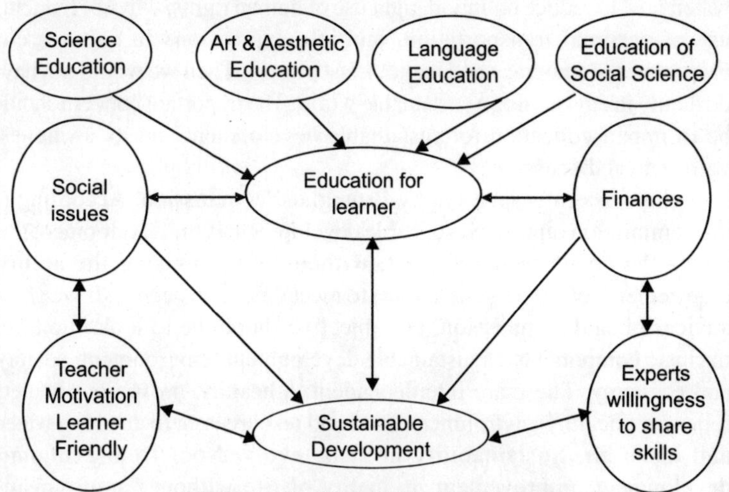

Scheme for Sustainable Development

Is sustainable development enough?

One may not compromise on only sustainable? Development should always be for growth. Every one strives for getting more knowledge, more wealth, more comfort, best of health, more appreciation from society as well as more security. To achieve all those development should be more than sustainable. The drawback being after culmination there may be sharp fall. This probably has been witnessed by the world between 600 AD to 1600 AD.

What is Worrying US?

> "The doctor has been taught to be interested not in health but in disease. What the public is taught is that health is the cure for disease."
> —*Ashley Montagu*

The learner at the school does not influence the parents. In the classroom the teacher impresses upon about different things including scientific attitude and values to a learner. This should go to parents. Parents also need to be blamed. In parent—teacher meeting school should ensure that parents are told about improving local environment. The meetings are a kind of ritual not for conviction. Just knowing is not enough. Ideas need to be implemented.

Our fervent task is that we should identify what is unsustainable in our societies. How efficient use of energy can happen, how to conserve water, how to reduce pollution, right use of human rights, whys of reducing use of personal transportation, multiple expressions in cultures etc. Everywhere democracy and justice must prevail. Then we would not have difficulty in envisioning a sustainable world. The important concern should be to impart education for sustainable development and its awareness with critical discussion.

The concern is spelt out by Brundtland commission. According to the commission report, "Sustainable development is the development that meets the needs of the present, without compromising the ability, requirements of future generations, to meet their own needs". If we go by advices of said commission, our objective should be to look into three intrinsic components of sustainable development: environment, society, and economy. These are interdependent: a healthy, prosperous society relies on a healthy environment, food and resources, safe drinking water, and clean air. Sustainability must be evolved out from economic development, improvement in quality of life without compromising environmental and societal commitment.

Are We Sailing Against the Wind?

"Research is what I'm doing when I don't know what I'm doing".
—Wernher von Braun

The answer should be yes! Why? The reason is whenever we go against prevailing practices then only new things are discovered. Every change has always been challenged and the person pursuing it is harassment. One shloka says '*vighne punha punarapi pratihanya mana prarbdhchyottam jana na parityajanti*', means great persons emerge out winner even after blockades one after the other.

Analyze following statements (whether there is a truth) and report if objectives are satisfactorily achieved.

Are we depriving a person trained in a skill to ignore the skill and do something else? Driver is educated to make safer travel.

Fire-safety education expects no fire tragedy whether it is life or property.

Surgical education is to make a person free from infected part and save life.

Teacher education is for making efficient teachers.

Vocational education makes the learner skilled/adept in the field in which she/he is trained.

Art education, calls for an art learnt, is displayed satisfactorily.

If the mason who built Tajmahal, ends up with hands cut on its completion (the story goes like that, this statement is subject to its validity). Is it O.K.?

The objective is that we must see that we make wind to allow us to sail in our desired direction. Education is for that.

Note: Earlier there were skilled boatmen who could make boat sail in desired direction, irrespective of the direction of the wind. Blind following is, however, not advocated. Hence we must seek a path which follows objectives of ESD are fulfilled.

ESD promises to make the world more liveable and safe for future generations. There may be a few abuses which distort ESD. It may be antithetical to the nature of ESD. Let us call for imparting people requisite knowledge and skills for lifelong learning and achieving the set goal.

Is Sustaining Development Enough?

> "Nevertheless, the concept of sustainable development is now known—even amongst those who haven't accepted it—and it's recognized, debated and followed by an increasing number of businesses".
>
> —*Maurice Strong*

At first place let us review global efforts for ESD (*see* Appendix). Efforts collectively taken by nations are: Environmental issues, Parity in living standards, Open economic system, Women participation and education which ultimately lead for better life and job conditions, Preservation of cultural identity, Promoting education, awareness and training, Resource consumption, Reorienting curriculum conducive for ESD, Creating job opportunities in greener industries, Compulsory education for children, Reduce migration from rural to urban cities for jobs by providing opportunities at different levels, Awareness for lifelong education, Implementation of decisions taken at wider plate form, Empower nations in decision making, Quality life for one and all etc.

> "The science of today is the technology of tomorrow."
>
> —*Edward Teller*

APPENDIX

"Whenever anyone says, 'theoretically,' they really mean, 'not really'."
—*Dave Parnas*

Excerpts from Various Net Cites Listed in References

The United Nations Conference on Environment and Development (UNCED), also known as the Rio Summit, Rio Conference, Earth Summit held in Rio de Janeiro from 3 June to 14 June 1992 was first of its own kind. The Rio Declaration on Environment and Development listed18 principles of sustainability. In these nations may avail some rights like- Nations have the sovereign right to exploit their own resources, but without causing environmental damage beyond their borders. Nations shall develop international laws to provide compensation for damage that activities under their control cause to areas beyond their borders. Nations shall use the precautionary approach to protect the environment. Where there are threats of serious or irreversible damage, scientific uncertainty shall not be used to postpone cost-effective measures to prevent environmental degradation.

Education for Sustainable Development (ESD) describes the practice of teaching for sustainability. In US it formed the first international document that identified education as an essential tool for achieving sustainable development and highlighted areas of action for education. In order to achieve sustainable development, environmental protection shall be an integral part of the developmental. Eradicating poverty and reducing disparities in living standards in different parts of the world are essential. Nations should reduce and eliminate unsustainable patterns of production and consumption, and promote appropriate demographic policies. Environmental issues are best handled with the participation of all concerned citizens. Nations shall facilitate and encourage public awareness and participation by making environmental information widely available. Nations shall enact effective environmental laws, and develop national law regarding liability for the victims of pollution and other environmental damage. Where they have authority, nations shall assess the environmental impact of proposed activities that are likely to have a significant adverse impact. Nations should cooperate to promote an open international economic system that will lead to economic growth and sustainable development in all countries. Environmental policies should not be used as an unjustifiable means of restricting international trade. The full participation of women is essential to achieve sustainable development. The creativity, ideals and courage of youth and the knowledge of indigenous people are needed too. Nations should recognize and support the identity, culture and interests of indigenous people. Peace, development and environmental protection are interdependent and indivisible. Sustainable development has three components: environment, society, and economy. If you consider the three to be overlapping circles of the same size, the area of overlap in the center is human well-being. As the environment, society, and economy become more aligned, the area of overlap increases, and so does human well-being. From the time sustainable development was first endorsed at the UN General Assembly in 1987, the parallel concept of education to support sustainable development has also been explored. From 1987 to 1992, the concept of sustainable development matured as committees discussed, negotiated, and wrote the 40 chapters of *Agenda 21.* Initial thoughts concerning ESD were captured in Chapter 36 of *Agenda 21,* "Promoting Education, Public Awareness, and Training." Unlike most education movements, ESD was initiated by people outside of the education community. In fact, one major push for ESD came from international political and economic forums (e.g., United Nations, Organization for Economic Co-operation and Development, Organization of American States). As the concept of sustainable development was discussed and formulated, it became apparent that education is key to sustainability. In many countries, ESD is still being shaped by those outside the education community. The concepts and content of ESD in these cases are developed by ministries, such as those of environment and health, and then given to educators to deliver. Conceptual development independent of educator input is a problem recognized by international bodies as well as educators.

Two of the major issues in the international dialog on sustainability are population and resource consumption. Increases in population and resource use are thought to jeopardize a sustainable future, and education is linked both to fertility rate and resource consumption. Educating females reduces fertility rates and therefore population growth. By reducing fertility rates and the threat of overpopulation a country also facilitates progress toward sustainability. The opposite is true for the relationship between education and resource use. Generally, more highly educated people, who have higher incomes, consume more resources than poorly educated people, who tend to have lower incomes. In this case, more education increases the threat to sustainability.

Implementation: An educated citizenry is vital to implementing informed and sustainable development. In fact, a national sustainability plan can be enhanced or limited by the level of education attained by the nation's citizens. Nations with high illiteracy rates and unskilled workforces have fewer development options. For the most part, these nations are forced to buy energy and manufactured goods on theinternational market with hard currency. To acquire hard currency, these countries need international trade; usually this leads to exploitation of natural resources or conversion of lands from self-sufficient family-based farming to cash-crop agriculture. An educated workforce is key to moving beyond an extractive and agricultural economy.

Decision making: Good community-based decisions—which will affect social, economic, and environmental well-being—also depend on educated citizens. Development options, especially "greener" development options, expand as education increases. For example, a community with an abundance of skilled labour and technically trained people can persuade a corporation to locate a new information-technology and software-development facility nearby. Citizens can also act to protect their communities by analyzing reports and data that address community issues and helping shape a community response. For example, citizens who were concerned about water pollution reported in a nearby watershed started monitoring the water quality of local streams. Based on their data and information found on the World Wide Web, they fought against the development of a new golf-course, which would have used large amounts of fertilizer and herbicide in maintenance of the grounds.

Quality of life: Education is also central to improving quality of life. Education raises the economic status of families; it improves life conditions, lowers infant mortality, and improves the educational attainment of the next generation, thereby raising the next generation's chances for economic and social well-being. Improved education holds both individual and national implications.

REFERENCES

http://www.unesco.org/new/en/education/themes/leading-the-international-agenda/education-for-sustainable-development/

http://ase.tufts.edu/gdae/

http://en.wikipedia.org/wiki/Education_for_Sustainable_Development

http://www.esdtoolkit.org/discussion/default.htm

http://www.brainyquote.com/quotes/quotes/w/wernhervon107615.html#ETtehe5Cs6J3OF2M.99

National Council on Science and the Environment and University Leaders for a Sustainable Future deliberated in groups to respond to the call by the UN General Assembly for a Decade of Education for Sustainable Development (2005 through 2014).

http://en.wikipedia.org/wiki/Archimedies

http://en.wikipedia.org/wiki/Earth_Summit

9

Education and Sustainable Development

An Exploration of the Linkages

Saumen Chattopadhyay and *Emon Nandi*

It is being increasingly felt world over supported by both empirical evidences and theoretical formulations that education plays a stellar role in spurring growth and achieving a broad-based economic development. In studies covering the growth of the world economy as a whole and a comparison of income growth across the nations, human capital has been identified as a significant factor in the emerging divergences in growth among the nations. It is not surprising as knowledge as an input to production of goods and services has become a prime mover of growth.

However, the improvement in the social indicators has not always been commensurate with the economic growth. The lack of correspondence has been found to be more profound in the context of the developing nations. For India, the differences in the ranking between the Human Development Index (HDI) and per capita income ranking in the world have become starker after India had achieved high growth rate in the recent years. It was admitted in the policy circle (GoI, *Economic Survey* 2010-11) that a higher rank in terms of per capita income than HDI could be attributed to unsatisfactory attainment in the realm of education. The linkage between growth and social development could be made stronger and robust only with steady improvement in attainment in education. But the question remains to be addressed is how does education matter for sustainable development?

Education and Growth

The linkage between education and growth has been empirically investigated quite extensively in the literature. The new growth theory investigates primarily the relationship between human capital and growth. Increase in productivity can not be explained merely in terms of a rise in effective labour force and capital. Technological change is crucial and it has been conceptualised in various ways. The new growth models (e.g., Lucas 1989, Romer 1990) made technological progress endogenous to the economic system and therefore it sought to explain why different nations witness different rates of technological progress[1]. It was argued that labour cannot be treated as homogenous over time as education and training made labour more and more skilled which led to an increase in productivity of labour. Since the concept of simple labour was no more tenable, it was replaced by the concept of human capital. Productivity enhancing education and training would remain embodied in human beings. It was a form of capital because education and training needed investment on education and training just like any other investment which leads to capital formation. Formation of human capital through skill formation and dissemination would contribute to innovation and technological advancement. The decision to spend on education and training was argued to be the fallout of optimizing decisions of the individual decisions to invest on human capital formation. This made possible the replacement of the constant returns to scale production function with diminishing productivity of capital as used by Solow by incorporating increasing returns to scale production function and externalities. Empirical studies have verified the role of human capital and knowledge in the growth process. It has policy implications in the sense that knowledge about technology and levels of information would make important contributions to the growth process and overall economic development (Olssen and Peters 2005) and the gaps between the nations in terms of development would be located in the gaps in knowledge base. The other forms of endogenous growth theoretic models is that of increasing returns to scale which may take various forms like economies of scale, learning by doing or the hypothesis that costs of innovation is independent of the size of the market but the rewards are proportional to it which spur innovations.

Endogenisation of the growth model is achieved by introducing the search for new ideas by the researchers who are interested in return from their investment in knowledge creation. Romer (1990) proposed three premises. One, an improvement in the instructions for mixing together raw materials is the core of technological change as raw materials remain unchanged, two, intentional actions taken in response to market incentives to develop ideas: academic scientists funded by the government are also to be considered along with research and development expenditures invested by the industry/corporate sector, and three, instructions for working with raw materials are different from conventional economic goods. Essentially what Romer (1990) argues that new ideas propel growth by way of reorganizing physical resources, natural, and human capital in a more efficient and productive manner (Peters and Besley, 2009).

While marginal cost (MC) of instruction created earlier being almost equal to zero as cost of replication is negligible mainly due to the advancement achieved in computer technology, fixed cost of creating that idea or instruction remains genuinely positive and substantial. This is the defining characteristic of technology. This makes economics of ideas different from economics of objects. Knowledge is different from other goods which are tradable in the market and it is pertinent to find out whether knowledge is a private or a public good.

Goods are classified on the basis of degree to which they are rivalrous and degree of excludability. As per the neoclassical definition, the public good has two main characteristics, the non-rivalry in consumption and non-excludability. The first feature means that the benefits of consumption accrue to many as consumption by one individual does not lead to a reduction in its availability for others[2]. Rivalry and excludability are often linked as the extent of non-rivalry leads to excludability. Rivalry in consumption is purely a technological attribute. However, excludability is a function of both technology and legal system, i.e., whether it is permissible to use, e.g., software, or, music CD. Technology is being classified as a non-rival input. Knowledge in its conceptual or immaterial forms (an idea or information or concepts) is argued to be non-rivalrous in consumption as an idea or a design or a formula could be used again and again without there being a decline in its usefulness. In fact with the use, a piece of knowledge may become more valuable with refinement and modification. But, if consumption benefits accrue to all, pricing becomes difficult as technically, it may not be feasible to exclude those who are not willing to pay. This leads to a failure of the market if exclusion is not feasible as people would prefer either to free ride (use knowledge for free) or would undervalue the benefit of knowledge deliberately to pay less for the product. However, if exclusion is feasible, exclusion of the user of the knowledge who is not willing to pay would not be an efficient outcome as transmission of knowledge would be virtually costless with marginal cost of provision to a consumer (MC) is negligible or zero.

Non-rivalry and partial excludability of knowledge made Economics of knowledge different from traditional economics of people with human beings with all their expertise, skills and strengths and capital natural resources and even financial assets (Peters and Besley 2009 quote Warsh 2006). Given non-rivalry of knowledge, often it is a matter of policy to make exclusion possible through codification and/or material embodiment and sell knowledge at a price. It requires some form of legal protection or patenting to give incentives to the producers of knowledge and recover the costs of knowledge production. However, knowledge in its conceptual form like a mathematical formula which is an input to research cannot be made generally patentable as ideally, not only it would seriously damage research and hinder the pace of innovation it is not excludable. Moreover, knowledge can generate extensive externalities paving the way for more innovations in other fields. Therefore, knowledge can ideally be argued to be a mixed good as the extent of 'publicness' becomes a matter of policy decision as the degree of excludability is subject to the discretion of the policy makers.

Education and Economic Development: Understanding the Linkages

Over the past years, the concept of development has changed from income oriented growth to human development and now to sustainable development (Comim, 2007). Drèze and Sen (1996: 10) defined the concept of economic development from a long term broader perspective[3].

> "One way of seeing development is in terms of the expansion of the real freedoms that the citizens enjoy to pursue the objectives they have reason to value, and in this sense the expansion of human capability can be, broadly, seen as the central feature of the process of development."

What people can do or can be, a process of emancipation from the enforced necessity to 'live less or be less'; whether they can live long, be well nourished, be able to read and write communicate, take part in literary and scientific pursuits. Capabilities reflect freedom which is necessary to achieve happiness. This entails command that people have over their lives. Deprivations (exploited landless labourer) are not captured in metric of utilities. Happiness is one of many capabilities but happiness by itself cannot be the sole indicator of all capabilities. For example, one may get good food but would feel constrained at every step to realise her potential.

Development is about structural changes, questioning the existing inequities and unfair practices. So the focus is neither on commodities, nor characteristics, nor utility, but a person's capability, on autonomous actions. It is not merely a compilation of 'functionings' to remain actively involved in shaping their own destiny and not the recipients of development programmes.

Development as Freedom: A New Concept of Development

If development as freedom is a challenge to the conventional approach where per capita income is central to development, then the question is to identify the essence of this paradigm and how does it compare with the traditional one. In the conventional approach, per capita income is measured and considered as a proxy for development. The underlying idea is that material well being yields satisfaction. Apart from concern for distribution, one, of course, needs to worry about externalities, existence of black economy, destruction of nature, and household work when we rely on income as the sole indicator of well being. When the nation grows, the expectation that trickle down would work also grows. But growth is not adequate even if we consider all other aspects related to the structure of the economy. There are issues which deter and inhibit an individual to realise the full potential of opportunities and earn income like gender discrimination or discrimination based on social categories, poor quality of public utilities and/or absence of rights and liberties. One needs access to other basic amenities of life and availability of goods and services so as to convert them to achieve a state of being. Mere availability of a consumption basket does not mean much. The question is what does one do with them? Our aim in life goes beyond mere consumption of goods and services. When we aspirc to live with dignity and seek to achieve a state of being, the challenge is to relate our aspirations to goods and services and our entitlement. To probe a little deeper, even entitlement is not sufficient as conversion depends on so many factors, socio-political-cultural as discussed above. Therefore, concepts of capabilities and freedom, equity and social justice, and skill formation assume salience in our striving for an achievement in our well-being. Therefore, this new approach is different from mere expansion of goods and services: growth in the conventional approach is a rise in per capita income and a concomitant rise in consumption and satisfaction. The value of goods and services depends on what they can do for people or what people can do with those goods and services. However, happiness or desire fulfilment is only one aspect of human existence. Traditional welfare economics is narrow and fundamentally inadequate for the study of holistic development and structural change. Deprivations and exploitation which are the defining features of a developing economy, are not reflected in this per capita income based approach to development. For example, giving food to somebody in prison or giving book to somebody illiterate would do little for their sense of freedom and attainment of a state they desire to be as Sen would like to argue.

Human Capital Versus Human Development

We need to distinguish between contributions of human agency in growth over and above contribution made by the accumulation of capital. The link between public action and economic progress becomes crucial.

It is about quality of human life and not just an instrument for promoting economic growth. There is asymmetry between human capital and physical capital. The former can have importance on its own. Being educated or healthy are valuables on their own even if they do not have any impact on income generation. Per capita income growth can be seen as merely instrumental. What does it do to our lives? Increase in income and a rise in life expectancy can come about through higher public spending and lowering the number of people below the poverty line. Growth mediated progress can be seen as growth mediation through public services and poverty removal.

Human Capability and Human Capital

In the context of his new approach to 'development as freedom', Drèze and Sen (1996) deliberate on his concept of human capability in contrast to the traditional concept of human capital. Though human agency is common to both the approaches, human capital focuses on skill formation and its influence on productivity and human earnings, whereas human capability focuses on the ability of the people to live life they have reason to value and to expand real choices they face in life. A distinction is made between direct and indirect valuation of achievements of human capability: direct and indirect. The former refers to direct impact on the individual in the form of better nourishment and better health. Indirect refers to the functioning which contributes to further production. Sen lists three roles of human capabilities (Sen 2000: 296) as (i) the direct role in terms of well-being and freedom of people; (ii) indirect role through influencing social change and (iii) indirect role through economic production.

Human capital concentrates more on the indirect effects and it is in this sense the approach is narrow. Human capital would imply only (iii) as mentioned above. It is however true that an increasing income would also help a person achieve freedom to an extent possible in other spheres of life. As Sen (2000: 296) puts it,

> "We must go *beyond* the notion of human capital, after acknowledging its relevance and reach. The broadening that is needed is additional and inclusive, rather than in any sense, an *alternative* to the 'human capital' perspective".

An increase in female literacy would not only reduce gender disparities in the society, it may reduce fertility, larger participation in the operation of local rural bodies. Basic education would also improve the functioning of the institutions, and informed public debates.

Role of Education in Development

Education is central to the capability approach and basic to all other capabilities. Absence of opportunities or lack of it can put an individual in a disadvantageous position irreversibly and forever. Further, this basic capability contributes towards expansion of all other capabilities including the future ones (Terzi 2007: 30). The notion of capability as implied, education has a much larger role to play for an individual and social development. Not only does it enhances well-being and freedom of individuals and peoples and contributes to economic production, education ushers in social change. If development is defined as an expansion of other capabilities and freedom, education occupies a central place. Social context and social relations can enlarge or constrain individual capabilities for education. Equality thus depends on personal responsibility for actions (effort). Material (goods and services) and non-material (effort) shape the opportunities that we have and the choices that we make. Education is viewed as a constitutive aspect of development. People are viewed as ends in themselves not as means to achieve. Education is not for efficiency and social welfare. But also for enjoying the culture, participate in activities and affairs, social and political, to provide each individual a secure sense of one's own worth.

Individual 'functionings' are influenced by a person's relative advantages in society and enabling public and policy environments (e.g., good teachers, productive peer relationships).

1. Intrinsic importance: valuable achievements in themselves. It can affect effective freedom directly.
2. Instrumental personal roles: seizing economic opportunities. Getting a job and earning which will affect achievement of other 'functionings'. After all, purchasing power is important. Education gives skill and it is easier for the person to sell in the job market.

3. Instrumental social roles: participation in public discussion of social needs, informed collective demands, improvement in public delivery of services and its better utilization.
4. Instrumental process roles: process of schooling can reduce child labour, social connectivity improves, improves horizon, e.g., 'Campus life'.
5. Empowerment and distributive roles: resist exploitation, organize politically to get a fairer deal, both within groups as well as within family. Female education is effective for gender based inequalities.

As Terzi (2007) argue that empirical research supports the role of education to the flourishing of individuals and their quality of life (*ibid.*: 32). Terzi quotes Schuller *et al.*(2004) that the important function of education is to enable people to have a sense of a future for themselves, for their families and communities and provides a kind of choice, opens up new vistas of life, extends the horizons of life hitherto unimagined. Sen along with Freire and Nussbam restores the humanistic view of education as opposed to the dominant modernist theories of education such as human capital theory, manpower planning or an idea of knowledge based economies (Flores-Crespo 2007: 48). Human beings are conceived of responsible agents who can carve out their own destinies.

Education and Externalities

Education generates benefits which spill over to the society called externalities in the parlance of economics. Non-rivalry in consumption is noting but externalities. It is in fact the most important defining characteristic of education from the perspective of economic theory which, to a large extent assume central place in the many of the debatable issues while education is subject to economic analysis. Externalities are cases of missing markets and hence valuation is extremely difficult. But that cannot be the reason to keep externalities out of economic analysis of education.

Externalities are to be distinguished from private non-market benefits beyond earnings such as health and quality of life. External benefits of education comprise many direct and indirect benefits. It can range from ensuring democratic functioning of the institutions, deepening of democracy, human rights to longevity, lower crime and corruption, to happiness and building up of social capital (McMahon 2010). The indirect external benefits of education are over and above these direct benefits.

The indirect benefits work through other variables and feedback over time to contribute towards private market and non-market benefits. The indirect benefits set the stage for higher growth in the present and for the future generations. This dynamics means present growth is also being contributed by past levels of education attainments and present education would also raise the future growth profile.

Locating Education in Sustainable Development

The concept of sustainable development cannot be understood within a single-dimension framework. It is a multi-dimensional concept whose main pillars are the environment, economy and society (Ashford and Hall 2011). The importance of the first pillar, i.e. environment needs no explanation, as this was the starting point of any discussion on sustainable development. The other two dimensions, economy and society are interrelated between themselves and with environment through various channels. This section explores some of the linkages and seeks to position education at the core of whole structure.

Education helps spreading awareness about the need to protect environment and can combat corrupt practices, which is the major source of degradation of nature. Environmental education makes individual understand the importance of nature and the need to distribute natural resources in a sustainable way. Research and development can develop eco-friendly technologies, which can be useful in sustaining the environment. Apart from this, in order to be sustainable, a development process should also ensure adequate and fair supply and distribution of basic amenities. It should encourage individuals within the society to fully realize the potentials of their abilities and get a fair reward in return. Economy, thus plays an important role in the development process and it is related with education as the latter enables individuals to be engaged in productive capacities in a meaningful way. Society, is another most important dimension of sustainable development. Education transforms individuals to socially responsible citizens. Thus, education actually resides at the core of all three dimensions of sustainable development. In other words, three pillars of sustainable development are very much inter-dependent and inter-related and education forms the very base of this pyramid (*see* Figure 9.1).

Now let us explore the operational linkages between the three pillars of sustainable development and the significance of education in more details. The three channels through which education binds environment,

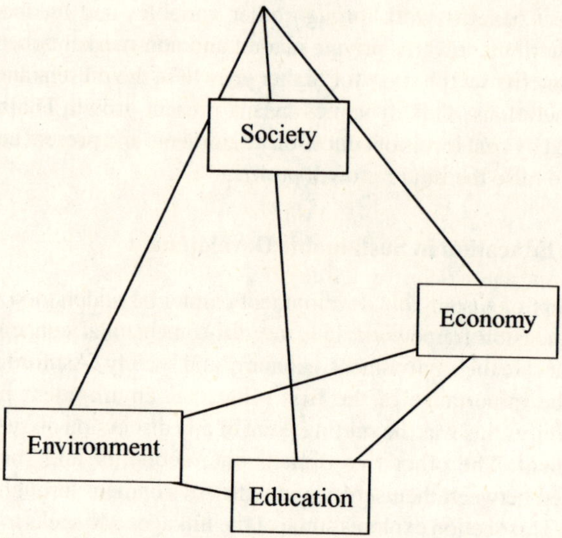

Fig. 9.1: Sustainable Development Pyramid and Education
Source: Based on Scoullos, 2010.

society and economy together are technology, governance and culture. However, each of these three linkages and their functioning are based on education.

The first perspective of implementing sustainable development is through technology. According to Ashford and Hall (2011), technology is the medium through which an economy interacts with the environment. Technology actually determines the way labour and capital are combined in the production system, and in turn, it also determines the nature of work, the conditions of earning livelihood, distribution of earnings *inter alia*. In the long run, the ability of an economy to deliver a decent level of material well-being to its citizens, thus, depend on technology. J.D. Bernal (1969), views a technique as 'an individually acquired and socially secured way of doing something'. However, there is indeed a gap between our understanding of doing something and actually making it work (Hirschman, 1967). Education plays a key role in narrowing this gap and making the work-force technologically advanced so that they can take part in the nation's growth process by getting employed in a meaningful and productive work. The three different aspects of employment are (i) the income aspect, (ii) the production aspect and (iii) the recognition aspect (Sen, 1975). Employment yields an output, and also enables an individual having fair and adequate purchasing power by means of providing fair wages, thus help in possessing command over essential goods and services. It also gives a person the 'recognition' that he or she is engaged in a meaningful worthwhile job (Sen, 1975). The current concept of development does not only focus on income as the only characteristic of development, employment remains at the core of any development process. Employment is that channel of economy, through which the benefits of an economic development accrues to the society and reduces inequality. At the same time, engagement in decent employment of a nation's labour force reduces the dependence on nature. Better knowledge about modern and safe technology can actually cause less harm to the environment and reduces the pollution. A shift towards an eco-friendly less-polluting production system through the adoption of new technologies thus can only be possible with the involvement of educated minds that can absorb these new techniques efficiently and productively. Thus, technology is a very important factor in ensuring a responsible economy for a sustainable development process.

Governance, the other important aspect of sustainable development, links the institution to the people and environment. To improve the sustainability of an economy and an environment, three things are important: (1) role of government (2) democratic decision making or public opinion, and, (3) collaboration among stakeholders. Government intervention in areas like education, health, energy supply, environmental issues, employment and labour management, etc., is essential for ensuring an inclusive, environment friendly and sustainable development process. Participatory democracy and civic engagement in decision-making can strengthen the role of welfare state and ensure that the distribution of resources is fair and just.

Education has immense externalities as mentioned in the last section. Apart from making individuals more productive and the nation to grow fast, education converts individuals into the responsible members of a civil society. Education enables an individual realizing the basic responsibilities, participating in the decision making process, and ensuing institutional mechanism to work in an efficient and just manner. Educationally trained minds can be engaged in the larger debates regarding justice, rights and responsibilities.

The third important channel is culture that influences the way individuals value the community, environment and the economic well-being. The role of 'tolerance' is imperative in order to address the cultural challenges of education for sustainable development. Culture and value-systems of a nation determine the way tensions between 'global' and 'local', 'universal' and 'individual', 'tradition' and 'modernity', 'competition' and 'equality', 'spiritual' and 'material', 'expression of knowledge' and 'capacity to assimilate', etc., are resolved (Scoullos, 2010).

Education inculcates values in individuals and thus helps in forming a distinct culture based on the value framework. It is fundamentally about the values and respect for past, present and future generations, for differences and diversity, and for the nature, environment and its resources (Scoullos, 2010). Education enables an individual in identifying her position with respect to the community, society and natural environment. In other words, education has the potentials of achieving a development process, which ensures a just, safe, healthy, environment-friendly and economically advanced society.

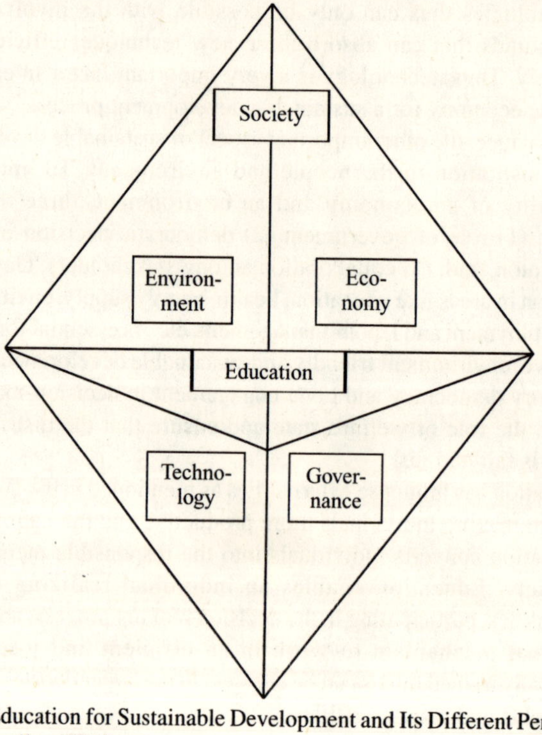

Fig. 9.2: Education for Sustainable Development and Its Different Perspectives
Source: Scoullos, 2010.

Summarizing the above discussion, it can be said that education is the base of the double sided pyramid whose upper facets are environment, economy and society. The three operational channels through which education helps in sustaining a development process are the lower facets of the pyramid, namely, technology, governance and culture.

Role of Education in the Era of Globalization

There are four channels through which sustainable development and globalization can be argued to be linked. They are the followings: (i) the production of goods and services (ii) the mobility of knowledge and information (iii) capital mobility and (iv) the international movement of labour and human resources, or migration (Ashford and Hall, 2011). Economy, environment, employment—the three main components of sustainable development actually get affected by technological innovation (Schumpeter, 1939) and globalized trade (Diwan and Walton, 1997; Etkins, Folke, *et al.*, 1994) and eventually globalization raises new challenges for governance, especially *vis-à-vis* the roles of government, workers, and the citizens in the new economic order (Ashford and Hall, 2011). Education, on the other hand, is closely related to globalization and sustainable development as it plays an essential role in shaping the nature of these inter-linkages. It plays a crucial role in this globalized era as countries are increasingly engaged in international competition of producing knowledge based on goods and services, especially for the absorption and transfer of knowledge and technology across countries (Amsden, 2002), and even for attracting foreign investment (Carnoy, 2009; Daun 2002). Moreover, education plays a stellar role in coping up with the changes and facing the challenges brought about by globalization and in ensuring a fair and just share of social and economic benefits to all (Carnoy and Castells, 2001; Green, 1997).

When the benefits emanating out of consumption transcend the international borders, the consumption does not remain confined to the territory marked by the international border of a nation. Education is no exception in this regard. Degrees obtained by cross-border foreign students, individualized status goods produced by nations are such examples. Foreign degrees in a way could be classified as global goods as these are the degrees obtained in border crossing and degree credentials which can be utilized in more than one nation in management, IT and scientific research (Marginson 2004). In the importing nations, commercial education implies extension of national educational capacity and individual student choice. Since foreign education is expensive, it reduces the 'publicness' by narrowing the size of the population. Other public goods are cross cultural, communications and understanding.

Global public goods can be defined as being characterised by 1. Non-rivalry and non-excludability; 2. Goods that are made broadly available across population on a global scale. Broadly available within countries, they are inter-generational, with no possible trade-off across the generations. At the same time, public 'bad' is cross-border pollutions. Global externalities arise from cross-border relationships and flows between the nations, HE is extensively and intensively networked, through research collaborations, e-mails, etc. Examples are knowledge in different fields, cross-border facilitations of cross-border recognition of universities, qualifications and individuals. Global public 'bads' are brain drain and the downside of cultural homogenization. Two way flows of personnel in the global higher education environment may be unequal as it leads to brain circulation. It can be global public 'bads' for some nations as it subtracts from the capacity to create as indicated by the prevailing stock of human capital at the national level. In an open global sphere, some nations lose out as they suffer flight of brains, other nations gain precious capital without dedicating resources for the production of the same. The same can be true for networks as some nations get excluded and some nations, generally the advanced ones, get included. Further, it is culturally asymmetrical as English language dominates. Developed countries are well placed to retain skill and infrastructure to access knowledge and the underdeveloped and the developing countries are not (Marginson *ibid.*).

There is no as such global policy space unlike a national economy as nations are autarkic and competing. However, global private goods are recognized. The overarching framework of WTO/GATS provides a negotiating framework for the participating nations. In this framework, higher education is treated as a tradable good as it is believed that nations would gain from trading of higher education as it is argued to be true for any other tradable good or service. Education, and in particular, higher education is treated as no different from any other tradable good or a service. As per the prevailing practice, there is hardly any consideration for free flow of knowledge across the borders and there is no need to align national recognition protocols, no consideration for public bads, gross unevenness between national educational systems.

The Issue of Fiscal Sustainability and Private Sector Participation

In the last sections, we have discussed how education could play a lead role to achieve a balanced development. However, to play such a role, education has to be considered largely as a public good to maximise the 'publicness' of education delivered. Though private participation in education can be encouraged as even historically, the private sector in education has been substantial and significant. What needs to be noted is to arrest the growing tendency to commercialise education provision. An enhanced role of the government entails an increased budgetary allocation for education. Of course, overcoming government failure will never be an easy job as corrupt practices are rampant in the Indian economy, society and polity. But corruption should not be an argument against government participation.

As discussed above, sustainability of any development process is a multi-dimensional one. Other than the traditional concern for environment, inclusive growth is crucial to sustainable development. Inclusive growth in the narrow sense requires that the income gains from rising production accrue to all the marginal sections of the society in a fair and just manner. The marginal sections need to participate in the economic activities to reap the benefits of productivity gains and participate in the decision-making process of the society in a democratic way to raise their voice against all attempts which seek to subdue their voice and curb their rights. Ensuring access to education is the first step for an inclusive growth. Ensuring education to all is a primary concern for any nation to achieve a development path which is sustainable.

It is an imperative that we have to deal with the policy issues to explore ways of realising the role of education in contributing to the process of sustainable economic development. How is education funded is intricately linked with the question of how is education delivered to the society. As we have tried to drive home the point that education and formation of human capital could be located at the centre of the agenda for development and in this scheme, the public sector has to play an important role. One reason behind limited intervention by the government has been the fiscal crunch. However, the allocation for primary education particularly under the head Sarva Siksha Abhiyan (SSA) has witnessed a rise. But the problem areas are, one, a high drop out rates; two, poor educational attainment. To put it differently, the challenges are to reduce the drop-out rates and effect an improvement in the quality of education. Without quality education, an increased budgetary allocation and the commensurate rise in the enrolment lose all its significance. One contention has been that the government should spend more and hence, the pertinent issue is whether the government has got the wherewithal to spend adequate resources on education. Implementation of the Right to

Education (RTE) Act is often argued to be constrained by fiscal constraint. What the government now needs to achieve is to raise the expenditure as a percentage of GDP to 6 per cent. Raising the expenditure by two percentage points is not a big deal if the government can devise tax strategy to phase out tax concessions without letting the tax-GDP ratio to fall further. Along with it, if tax evasion is curbed, resources constraint will cease to matter for the government.

Relying on the private sector to expand the education sector at all levels is not a good option for the government. The private sector driven by generation of even reasonable surplus will affect the access when the demand for education is going to originate from the growing aspirations of the under-privileged section of the society. The private sector requires a market like economic environment to flourish. The basic rationale behind the Bills being contemplated by the government is to create a regulated market which has to be eventually integrated with the global economy. The basic contention that private sector is more efficient and market is the best institution to guide allocation of resources and reform of the education sector is often untenable. Quality of education is not guaranteed unless there is in place a strict quality assurance mechanism and that too, it will only be the first step.

Concluding Remarks

The notion of development has eventually broadened from the narrow concept of income based growth to the capability based human development approach, and from there to the most recent idea of sustainable development. Education keeps on playing the central role in all these versions of development theories. Education and skill embedded in human beings in terms of human capital makes individuals more productive (Schultz 1961, Becker 1964) and increases competitiveness of the nation as a whole. The new growth theories (e.g., Romer, 1990) consider 'idea' as a major determinant of economic growth. Education, is also at the root of Sen's capability approach as it plays a major role in converting the capabilities into 'functionings' and help achieve freedom as the most important manifestation of development.

Sustainable development is a multi-dimensional concept based on three pillars—environment, economy and society. Education capable of generating a wide variety of externalities should be placed at the core of the three pillars of sustainable development. The three pillars of sustainable development are inter-related and inter-dependent through three channels—employment, governance and culture. Education is again at the centre of all these operational channels. Therefore, education deserves a central position in sustainable development framework.

Market based private sector participation may not be the best way to achieve sustainable development as the very participation of the private sector will compromise with inclusiveness of the growth process and would weaken the linkages between economy and the society.

By policy design the 'publicness' of education has to be enhanced. The government has to play a larger role. It is not easy as the public sector has not been able to deliver quality education. The stress has to be more on cooperation at the global level which is to be posited as an alternative to the neo-liberal framework and strengthening of the school education system.

NOTES

1. In Solow's model of growth, technical progress is exogenously given. Since investment decisions particularly in their formation of human capital are taken by the optimizing individuals, the new growth models are called endogenous models.
2. Subject to the congestion as beyond a limit congestion may reduce the benefit available.
3. It was originally Amartya Sen (1985) who introduced the new approach to view development in the form of expansion of capabilities.

REFERENCES

Amsden, A. (1992). *Asia's Next Giant: South Korea and Late Industrialisation*, New York: Oxford University Press.

Ashford, Nicholas A. and Ralph P. Hall edited (2011). *Technology, Globalization, and Sustainable Development: Transforming the Industrial State*, New Haven and London: Yale University Press.

Becker, Gary (1964/1975). *Human Capital: A Theoretical Analysis with Special Reference to Education*, New York: Columbia University Press.

Bernal, J.D. (1969). *Science in History,* Harmondsworth: Penguin.

Carnoy, M. and Castells, M. (2001). 'Globalisation, the Knowledge Society and the Network State: Poulantzas at the Millennium,' *Global Networks*, 1: 1-18.

Carnoy, Martin (2005). *Globalization, Educational Trends and the Open Society*, OSI Education Conference 2005: "Education and Open Society: A Critical Look at New Perspectives and Demands", Open Society Institute.

Comim, Flavio (2007). 'Concepts of Development: The role of education' in David Bridges, Palmira Juceviciene, Robertas Jucevicius, Terence

Mclaughlin and Jolanta Stankeviciute (edited) *Higher Education and National Development*, Routledge.

Diwan, I. and M. Walton (1997). Etkins, Folke, *et al.* (1994). 'How International Exchange, Technology and Institutions Affect Workers: An Introduction', *World Bank Economic Review*, 11(1), 1-15.

Daun, H. (edited) (2002). *Educational Restructuring in the Context of Globalisation and National Policy*, London: Routledge/Falmer.

Drèze, Jean and Amartya Sen (1996). *India: Economic Development and Social Opportunity*, Delhi: Oxford University Press.

Flores-Crespo, Pedro (2007). 'Situating Education in the Human Capabilities Approach', in Melaine Walker and Elaine Unterhalter (eds.) *Amartya Sen's Capability Approach and Social Justice in Education*, New York: Palgrave Macmillan.

Green, A. (1997). *Education, Globalisation and the Nation State*, Basingstoke: MacMillan.

Hirschman, A.O. (1967). *Development Projects Observed*, Brookings, Washington.

Lucas, Robert, E. Jr. (1988). 'On the Mechanics of Economic Development', *Journal of Monetary Economics*, July, 22(1), 3-42.

Marginson, Simon (2004). 'Competition and Markets in Higher Education: A 'Glonacal' Analysis', *Policy Futures in Education*, Vol. 2, No. 2, 175-244.

Marginson, Simon (2004). 'Australian Higher Education: National and Global Markets' in Pedro Teixeira, Ben Jongbloed, David Dill and Alberto Amaral (eds.), *Markets in Higher Education: Rhetoric or Reality?*, Dordrecht/Boston/London: Kluwer Academic Publishers.

McMahon, W.W. (2010). 'The External Benefits again of Education', in D.J. Brewer, and P.J. McEwan (eds.), *Economics of Education*, UK and USA: Elsevier and Academic Press.

Olssen, Mark and Michael Peters (2005). 'Neo-liberalism, Higher Education and the Knowledge Economy: From the Free Market to Knowledge Capitalism', *Journal of Education Policy*, 20 (3): 313-46.

Peters, Michael A. and Tina (A.C.) Besley (2009). 'Academic Entrepreneurship and the Creative Economy', in Michael A. Peters, Simon Marginson, and Peter Murphy (eds.), *Creativity and the Global Knowledge Economy,* Peter Lang, New York, pp. 71-89.

Romer, Paul J. (1990). 'Endogenous Technological Change', *Journal of Political Economy*, Vol. 98, No. 5, pp. S71 to S101.

Schultz, T. (1961). 'Investment in Human Capital', *American Economic Review*, 51, pp. 1-17.

Schumpeter, J.A. (1939). *Business Cycles: A Theoretical, Historical, and Statistical Analysis of the Capitalist Process*. New York: McGraw-Hill.

Scoullous Michael J. (2010). 'Education for Sustainable Development: The Concept and its Connection to Tolerance and Democracy' in Anastasia Nikolopoulou, Taisha Abraham and Farid Mirbagheri (eds.), *Education for*

Sustainable Development: Challenges, Strategies, and Practices in a Globalizing World, New Delhi: Sage.

Sen, Amartya (1975). *Employment, Technology and Development*, Oxford University Press, UK.

Sen, Amartya (1985). *Commodities and Capabilities*, Amsterdam: North-Holland.

Sen, Amartya (2000). *Development as Freedom*, Delhi: Oxford University Press.

Solow, Robert M. (1956). 'A Contribution to the Theory of Economic Growth', *Quarterly Journal of Economics,* 70, pp. 65-94.

Terzi, Lorella (2007). 'The Capability to Be Educated', in Melaine Walker and Elaine Unterhalter (eds.) *Amartya Sen's Capability Approach and Social Justice in Education*, New York: Palgrave Macmillan.

Warsh, D. (2006). *Knowledge and the Wealth of Nations*. New York: W.W. Norton.

10

Developing Sustainable Consciousness

Problem of Teacher Education

Debdulal Dutta Roy

Aim of the teacher education is development of sustainable consciousness within students in order to acquire knowledge, skill and to develop values necessary in shaping the future. Here shaping future means balanced adaptation into the social, political, economic and environmental changes. Sustainable education occurs when students can protect themselves and others by using gadgets through first-aid after learning about it. Sustainability develops motivation to do experiment with learnt materials. By learning photosynthesis, students can classify the plants that need more and less sunlight by doing different experiments on plants. Later on, this observation is applied in farming different kinds of plants. School education should engineer the syllabus and teaching pedagogies, infrastructure and reading and writing values in such a manner so that human consciousness will be motivated to understand rapid changes in surroundings and to develop different adaptive strategies in economic, social, political and cultural life.

Consciousness

Consciousness refers to one's experience about the surroundings. Experience occurs at each layer of consciousness. By the analysis of the songs of Rabindranath Tagore and the works of Rishi Aurobindo, author identified three layers of consciousness. These are *Murta*, *Raag* and *Saraswat*. When stimulus lies at the murta, individual experiences it's morphological characteristics. When it lies at the raag layer, one experiences affective value. And when it lies at the saraswat layer, individual experiences totality and harmony (Dutta Roy, 2006).

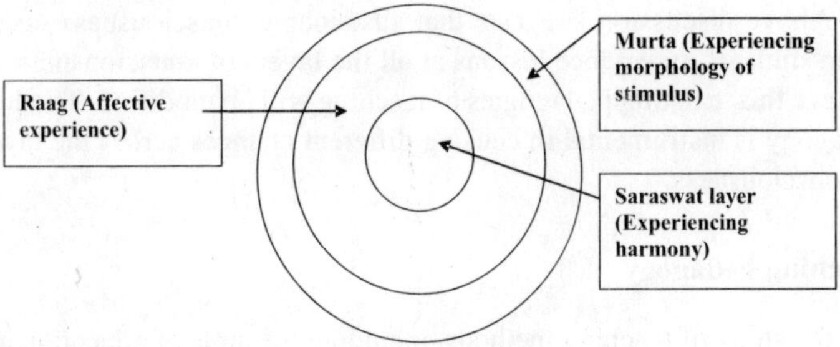

Fig. 10.1: Layers of Consciousness

When it rains, three girls of similar age groups are asked to share their experiences about rain. One says – "raining". 2nd girl says- "nice raining". And 3rd girl says – "dancing". Why does third girl avoid the word 'rain'? Has she not experienced rain ? Is there any ambiguity in her experience? Actually, she experiences rain and enjoys. But her experience is not limited to it's shape, pattern of falling, it's beauty rather she experiences it's total properties. Therefore, she experiences harmony of her imaginations, feelings with rain. This feeling of harmony leads to formation of new experience, i.e., dance.

During teaching, teachers give importance on morphological characteristics—spelling, vocabulary, pronunciation but not to the inner experience. Inner experience is important for sustainable development of our consciousness. It motivates students intrinsically to learn the lessons. After learning photosynthesis, one is searching other behaviour of plants. This effort is motivation to saraswat layer. Student does not forget the text when it reaches at the saraswat layer (Figure 10.2). This memory helps student to improvise learnt materials in adaptation.

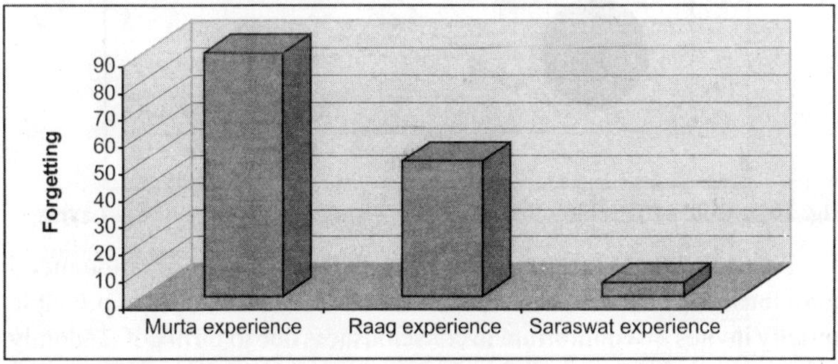

Fig. 10.2: Hypothetical Model About Forgetting Probability Across Three Layers

Above discussion suggests that sustainable consciousness occurs when students experience lessons at all the layers of consciousness. To achieve this, existing pedagogies of teaching will be modified. Teaching pedagogy is instrumental in causing different changes across the layers of consciousness.

Teaching Pedagogy

It is the study of teaching methods, including the aims of education and the ways in which such goals may be achieved. Pedagogy is the only tool that helps in changing three layers of consciousness over the time.

For sustainable development, there will be two levels of pedagogy. Level 1 is meant for change in Murta and Raag layer and Level 2 is for change in saraswat layer of consciousness.

Level 1 pedagogy involves observation, dreaming, playing, play therapy, drawing, story telling, touring, performing arts, phoneme competency Development. Level 2 includes conceptual conflict, creating classroom climate for questioning, generating curiosity, modelling, drilling, and generalization.

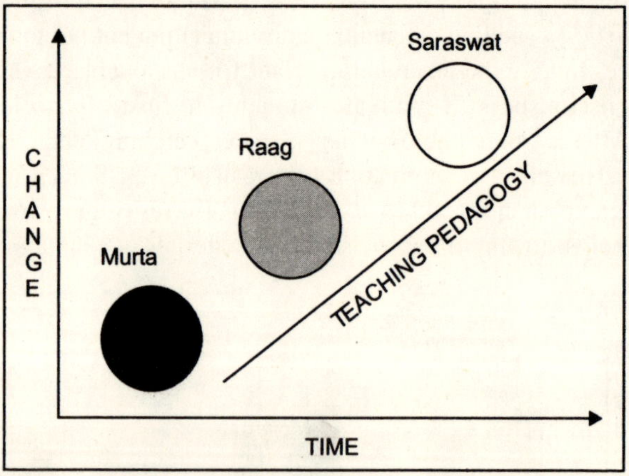

Fig. 10.3: Role of Teaching Pedagogy on Changes in Consciousness Layers

At each level, teaching should follow principle of unbounded consciousness, i.e., freedom to learn. Unbounded consciousness principle initially invites disequilibrium in consciousness due to influx of randomly processed information. Individual after experiencing all the information establish relation among all the layers and gradually the disequilibrium state lessens.

Some teaching pedagogies facilitating unbounded consciousness are discussed below:

***Inductive-deductive*:** Induction is the form of reasoning in which a general law is derived from a study of particular objects or specific processes. Students use measurements, manipulations or constructive activities and patterns to discover a relationship. They later formulate a law or rule about that relationship based on their observation, experiences, inferences and conclusions. Here, it must be cautioned to note that this pedagogy may be followed after concrete operational stage of intellectual development as suggested by Piaget. According to Piaget, children at the age of concrete operational stage can incorporate inductive but deductive logic which involves using a general principle to predict the outcome of a specific event.

Heuristic Method

Discovery through inquiry. It organizes investigation of real world phenomena into four steps:

- Wondering
- Designing
- Investigating
- Discovering

Project Method

It aims to bring practically designed experiences into the classroom. Often conducted over a period of three to six months. It can be given individually or in team. There are some parts of the curriculum in which children can work more independently. It acts as the complementary of the learning opportunities.

***Think-Pair-Share*:** It aims at thinking alone and later sharing with others before setting final answer. It provides higher level thinking and socialization.

It can be provided in small (three or four students) and large groups. The group can be formed formally or informally. Often this group discussion "sharing" is followed up with a larger classroom discussion. Some think-pair-share activities are short, "quick-response think-pair-share" and sometimes the activities may be longer and more involved, "extended think-pair-share." The instructor can use the student responses as a basis for discussion, to motivate a lecture segment, and to obtain feedback about what students know or are thinking and it is easy to incorporate more than one think-pair-share activity in a given class period.

***Performing Art*:** Teaching subject in association with performing art specially, dance, drama, music, songs, painting, sculpture act upon three layers of consciousness. Performing art provides imagination related to the text that enhances intrinsic motivation to read or to write. It promotes sensory-motor integration and coordinated movement. Coordinated movement fosters systematic cognitive growth. Second they enlighten consciousness by freedom of thinking. One student is given a picture of river. By seeing the picture, student pastes one quotation of Rabindranath Tagore on the picture.

Fig. 10.4: Associating Text with Picture and Changing Theme

Associating text with the performing art creates motivation to learn. One student instead of reading text spends more time in viewing cartoons in TV. The performing art therapist assigns names of her favourite cartoon character to the character of hero and heroine in the text. Suddenly, inattentive student finds interest to read the book. Through performing art, students learn how to regulate consciousness. They can convert noise into musical notes using performing art.

Performing art especially music is related to mathematics. Mathematics and music are related in the brain from very early in life (Burack, 2005). Musical elements such as steady beat, rhythm, melody, and tempo possess inherent mathematical principles such as spatial properties, sequencing, counting, patterning, and one-to-one correspondence. Thinking about relationships, such as bigger, smaller and faster, slower, and especially about pattern relationships, plays a special role in young children's mathematical development. Ayfer (2009) examined the effects of mathematics course that were supported by using songs on students' attitudes, achievements and multiple intelligences. In this study pre test-post test experimental design with control group and time series design were used. Sample of the study was composed of 286 third graders at primary schools. Scale of Attitudes towards Mathematics, Mathematics Achievement Tests for 5 units, Multiple Intelligences Inventory for Students were used as data collecting instruments. In this research meaningful differences in favour of experimental groups on attitudes towards and mathematics success in pre test post test comparisons were obtained.

School plays important role on sustainability of the consciousness. But this can not be achieved without school attendance motivation. Here is a study how attitudes toward school infrastructure can predict changes in motivation to attend the school.

Infrastructure and School Attendance Motivation

Infrastructure is recognized by all to be the major bottleneck to development (Rao, 2005). Dr. Manmohon Singh, the prime minister of India, recently gave major thrust on infrastructure facilities in education. He asserted "While growth generates wealth, we also need to invest in equitable social and physical infrastructure, catering to the needs of marginalized sections of our society which still need to catch up with the more advanced regions" (PM Reviews Mid term appraisal, 2005). Physical infrastructure, information sharing infrastructure, location of schools etc. are critical to learning experience of students. School buildings that can adequately provide a good learning environment are essential for student success (United States Department of Education, 2000). Professionals involved in school design assumed that as long as certain minimum standards for size, acoustics, lighting and temperature were met, a productive environment existed and teaching and learning would proceed normally (Conners, 1982; Cash, 1993; Berner, 1993). More recent research has determined that the physical environment and the learning experience can not be separated and are considered to be integral parts of each other (Taylor and Gousie, 1988). Pucca buildings are good enough for controlling temperature, acoustic quality or noise. Electricity, toilet and drinking water facilities and adequate number of class rooms are some of the basic physical infrastructures for academic achievement. No school can survive without sharing their values, mottos, and achievement of students to the neighboring people or the extending environment. School magazine and school exhibitions are the few outlets through which people of neighboring areas are aware of school functioning. Therefore, school maintains some information sharing infrastructure through which both schools and its surroundings can share information with each other. School library, magazine, school exhibition are some of the strategic measures for information sharing. Library plays critical role in improving academic achievement. Becker (1970) compared IOWA test of Basic skills scores between students in elementary schools with and without libraries and found that the presence of library and the guidance of librarian appeared to exert significant influence on pupil achievement in some information gathering skill areas. Both school magazine and exhibition are considered as major outlets to express creative abilities of students to the people. Distance of schools from main roads, market place and health centers is critical factor for the good school administration. Road connects rural schools with the city. Market place helps school to meet up its daily needs. And health center provides emergency care to the students, teachers and staffs of the school. Here is a study to examine attitude towards school infrastructure and motivation to attend the school.

Attitude

Throughout the history of psychology, the notion of attitude has played an essential role in the explanation of behaviour. Gordon Allport (1954), an early pioneer in attitude research, characterized the concept of attitude as distinctive and indispensable to social psychology. He defined attitude as a mental and neural state of readiness, organized through experience, exerting a directive or dynamic influence upon the individual's response to all objects and situations with which it is related.

Assessing attitude is complex as it is an unobservable hypothetical construct. It must be inferred from measurable responses indicating positive or negative evaluations of the attitudinal object. It may be inferred from three basic components. All three are related, and more they are consistent with each other the more stable is the attitude.

The *cognitive component* consists of the person's thought process, perceptions and beliefs, and evaluations about the attitude object. For example, students may think that school provides adequate space to sit in the classroom.

The *affective component* gives an emotional or feeling aspect to the attitude which, results in an object being liked or disliked. In the example of adequate space in above, student may feel warmth or liking for the school.

The *behavioural component* refers to the tendency to act towards the object in a consistent and characteristic way. Again, following the above example, student may want to attend the class regularly.

There are five basic characteristics of attitude. These are:

Valence: It is the degree of positive or negative feeling about an attitude object that predicts what attitude scales normally measure.

Centrality: It is the extent to which an attitude is a part of a person's self-concept and reflects the individual's identity.

Interrelatedness: It is the extent to which an attitude is related to a person's other attitudes.

Stability: It is simply an attitude's resistance to change.

Salience: It is a person's conscious awareness of the attitude.

Study: Current study focused on nine attitudes towards infrastructure as cleanliness, safety, comfort, adequacy, exploring, reliable, easiness, equal opportunity and willingness to participate in school activities. The definitions and assumptions behind each attitudinal variable are given below:

Cleanliness: Cleanliness is the absence of dirt, including dust, stains, bad smells and clutter. Purpose of cleanliness includes to make school free from offensive odor, dirt and contamination of germs and of diseases. Classrooms become dirty due to unused papers, wastage materials of tiffin-box, dusts coming through windows and doors etc. Good cleaning habit among students is important for classroom cleanliness. Brooming and washing are common means to make classroom clean. Clean classroom and toilet are healthy for the students. It protects students from diseases and germs. Students before starting class usually clean the classrooms with brooms. In some schools, sweepers are available for cleaning the classroom and toilets. Clean classroom, toilet, mid day meal, medical check up is assumed to affect student's motivation to attend school.

Like classroom, fresh and clean water is important in school. Clean water means absence of toxic substance. Presence of toxicity can be understood through foul smell, turbidity, unwanted colour etc. The main source of water is rainfall. In West Bengal, the state is endowed with large ground water sources. It is tapped by means of heavy and medium duty tube wells. Schools are allocated with such tube wells. Following Human Development Report of West Bengal, 2004, 83.2 per cent of habitations are under rural water management.

Safety: Safety is the state of being "safe" (from French *sauf*), the condition of being protected against any failure, damage, accident, errors or harms. Some of the safety systems in school are pucca building, covered electrical wares, safe drinking water, no slippery in toilet, wall-fixed blackboard, clean food and careful health check up. School maintains several safety systems to protect students like keeping emergency phone numbers, first aid kit, fire extinguishing cylinders.

Comfort: Comfort refers to feeling of pleasurable ease, a state of being relaxed and feeling of no pain. Feeling of comfort in learning at classroom and in uses of different infrastructures makes students at ease and relaxed.

Easiness: Like comfort, easiness plays important role in forming attitude towards school infrastructures. Easiness refers to posing no difficulty. Answering or asking questions to teachers with fear, difficulty to learn lessons, to take teacher's note or to follow teaching learning materials cause feeling of uneasiness in students.

Adequacy: Adequacy refers to feeling of sufficiency to satisfy a requirement or to meet a need. Adequate sitting position, illumination in classroom, drinking water, privacy in toilet use make students motivated towards school.

Exploring: It refers to systematic searching, examining or investigating. Students through learning process in classroom tend to explore the surroundings. Teachers, books, teaching learning materials play critical role in development of exploring attitude.

Reliability: It refers to dependability or consistency. Reliability on teachers, friends and textbooks develop interpersonal trust and good teacher-student interaction. It motivates students to attend the school regularly.

Equal opportunity: School infrastructure should be easily accessible to all the students. There should not be any prejudice or discrimination based on race, colour, age, gender, national origin, religion, mental or physical disability in participation of school sports, cultural programme, accessing books and in getting mid-day meal.

Willingness to participate in school activities: If there would be equal opportunity for access of infrastructures, students will be interested to participate in sports, cultural programmes, mid-day meal and health check up programme. They will be willing to attend the school regularly.

One 68-items questionnaire with 'Yes' and 'No' response categories was constructed to assess attitude towards school infrastructures. The questionnaire was administered to 572 students of primary schools from 12 rural blocks in 6 districts of West Bengal. The questionnaire had questions related to 9 attitudes—cleaning, safety, comfort, adequacy, exploring, reliability, easiness, equal opportunity and willingness to participate. there were 13 school infrastructure based questions. They were Classroom, blackboard, teaching, book, mid-day meal, drinking water, toilet, friend, book bank, health checkup, teaching learning materials, games, cultural programmes.

Infrastructures: Following principal component analysis, infrastructures are classified into 3 types—basic, supportive and activity based infrastructures. Basic infrastructure is composed of perception to classroom, blackboard, teaching, text book and mid-day meal. These 5 variables in together accounted for 23 per cent variance [R2 = 0.23, F(5,567) = 33.74, p<.000]. Mid-day meal [beta(567) = 0.28, p<0.00], text book[beta(567) = 0.15, p<0.00] and teaching [beta(567) = 0.16, p<0.00] predicted independently school attendance motivation.

Supportive infrastructure is composed of perception to Drinking water, Toilet, Friend, Book bank, and Health checkup facilities. Out of 5 infrastructures, perception to friend[beta(567) = 0.19, p<0.00], health checkup [beta(567) = 0.16, p<0.00], and toilet facilities [beta(567) = 0.16, p<0.00], predicted independently school attendance motivation Book bank and drinking water facilities can not predict school attendance motivation.

Activity based infrastructure is composed of TLM, Games and Cultural programmes. In correlating these 3 variables, it is noted that Games (r(571) = 0.33, p<0.00) and Cultural programmes (r(571) = 0.24, p<0.00) are more significantly and positively related to school attendance motivation than perception of TLM (r(571) = 0.09, p<0.03).

Attitude

It is noted that linear combination of 4 variables (Easiness, Willingness to Participate, Exploring, Safety) out of extracted 5, predict changes in school attendance motivation. In together, they accounted for 25 per cent (R2 = 0.25, F(5,567) = 37.80, p<.000) variance of predicted variable. This suggests that students like infrastructures that can be controlled easily, safe and exploring. Their willingness to participate in different school programmes motivates them to attend school. It indicates role of activity based infrastructure perception predicted (beta(569) = 0.24, p<0.00) more school attendance motivation when other variables were controlled.

To sum up, school attendance motivation facilitates sustainability of consciousness. And again, it depends on the attitude towards school infrastructure. Students want to perceive school infrastructure as more easy to understand, to explore, to feel comfort, exploring, safe to use and it must elicit willingness to participate into it. When above is fulfilled, students find interest to attend the school which is instrumental to develop sustainable consciousness; arrangement of activity based infrastructure motivates more to attend the school.

Reading and Writing Values

Values are the predispositions in our life. Sustainable consciousness is developed out of reading and writing values. Therefore, teacher should pay much attention to the value engineering. Each individual maintains hierarchical structure of values. And it is reflected in actions. Some students pay much attention to recognition values and they prefer reading and writing in order to be recognized by others. One has creative value and draws the picture when answering any question. It is the role of teacher to explore the reading and writing values of the students and to engineer them in such a manner so that the positive values can be facilitated in sustainable development of consciousness. For example, students having high recognition values can be engineered to the self recognition values for mastery over task or assignment. And students having creative values can be motivated to express creativity in writing wall magazine or school magazine. Creative students will be given some platforms so that their talents can be facilitated in a proper way. Through the analysis of lyrics or script of *Geetbitan*, Dutta Roy (2011) has noted 14 path and 14 goal oriented values. Path oriented values include 14 values as self-awakening, emotional control, developing positive power or energy, systematic, fearless, cleanliness, no work-family conflict, *niskam* principle, challenging, self-understanding, self-power, doubtless, free from fear of failure, advancement, altruism. There are 14 goal oriented values as peace, universalization, enlightenment, positive feeling, and family security, sense of accomplishment, pleasure, inner harmony, self-respect, salvation, self-empowerment, altruism, national security, and significance in life. During teaching, teacher will pay attention to the structure of path and goals oriented values within students and later direct the students accordingly.

Summing up, aim of education is development of sustainable consciousness in order to make students more adaptive, creative and innovative. This can be achieved through different teaching pedagogies, changing attitude of school infrastructure and engineering the value structure.

REFERENCES

Allport, G.W. (1954). Attitudes in the History of Social Psychology. In G Lindzey and Aranson (Eds), *Handbook of Social Psychology*, Vol. 1, Reading, MA: Addison-Wesley.

Ayfer Kocaba° (2009). Using songs in mathematics instruction: Results from pilot application Original Research Article Procedia—*Social and Behavioural Sciences*, 1, 1, 538-543

Becker, D.E. (1970). Social Studies Achievement of Pupils in Schools with Libraries and Schools Without Libraries. Unpublished doctoral dissertation, University of Pennsylvania.

Berner, M.M. (1993). Building conditions, parental involvement and student achievement in the district of Columbia Public School System. *Urban Education*, 28, 1, 6-29.

Burack, J. (2005). "Uniting Mind and Music: Shaw's Vision Continues." *American Music Teacher*, 55, 1, 84-87.

Cash, C.S. (1993). Building condition and student achievement and behaviour. *Unpublished doctoral dissertation*, Virginia Polytechnic Institute and State University.

Conners, D.A. (1982). The school's designed environment implications for understanding stress. *CEFPI's Educational Facility Planner*, 20 (1), 4-6.

Dutta Roy, D. (2003). Development of the questionnaire for assessment of reading and writing motivation of boys and girls of grades III and IV. *Unpublished project report, Indian Statistical Institute, Kolkata.*

Dutta Roy, D. (2006). A study on preferences to different reading and writing motives of tribal children in primary education of Tripura and Manipur. Unpublished project report, Indian Statistical Institute, Kolkata.

Dutta Roy, D. (2006). Development of picture drawing test to assess consciousness layers of tribal children of Tripura, *Journal of the Indian Academy of Applied Psychology*, Vol. 32, No. 1, 20-25.

Fowler, A.E. (1991). How Early Phonological Development might Set the Stage for Phonemic Awareness. In S. Brady and D. Shankweiler (Eds.), *Phonological Process in Literacy. A tribute to Isabelle Y. Liberman* (pp. 97-117), Hillsdale, NJ: Erlbaum.

PM Reviews Mid-term Appraisal, *Yojana*, 49, 41-42, 2005.

Rao, S.L. (2005). Use of forex reserves. *Yojana*, 49, 5-8.

Reeve, J. (1996). *Motivating Others: Nurturing Inner Motivational Resources. Needham Heights.* MA: Allyn and Bacon.

Taylor, A. and Gousie, G. (1988). The Ecology of Learning Environments for Children. *CEFPI Journal*, 26(4), 23-28.

UNESCO. (1993). *World Education Report*, Paris.

United States Department of Education. (April 3, 2000). Impact of inadequate school facilities on student learning.

World Bank. 1993. *The East Asian Miracle: Economic Growth and Public Policy* New York: Oxford University Press.

Ziegler, J.C. and Goswami, U. (2005). Reading Acquistion, Developmental Dyslexia, and Skilled Reading Across Languages: A Psycholinguistic Grain Size Theory. *Psychological Bulletin*, 31, 3-29.

11

Strategies in Higher Education for Sustainable Development

Some Approaches

Sima Pal

Education is an essential tool for achieving sustainability. People around the world recognize that current economic development trends are not sustainable and the key to moving society toward sustainability are public awareness, education and training. Education is the most powerful instrument which can moisten human being with knowledge, skill and capability to observe and analyze the sense of purpose and confidence for building a dynamic vibrant, joint and cohesive nation able to take care of its entire people. There are three stages of education—elementary, secondary and Higher education (College and University level).

Higher education occupies a place of special importance because it can provide ideas and personnel to give shape to the further and also sustain all the levels of education. Higher education is the place where knowledge—seeking people pilgrimage and for which they take time of their activities to widen their intellectual horizons (Noam, 1995).

The higher education system in India has grown in an outstanding way in the post independence period. Education system of India was a rich repository of culture and expressions fulfilling a human being's needs to communicate, to express and relate to others. Every community and region has its own means of expression in a variety of forms and these continue to play a role within the social group (Mahapatra, Anuka, 2010). However, the system is being devoured with many issues at present, as issues of training, management, knowledge, reorientation of programmes for laying emphasis on values and ethics as one of technology and quality of higher education.

The higher education system in India focuses many challenges. There is an immediate need to create some system to address these challenges. Higher education inter-relations among the social, political, technological and economic forces of the society.

"Peace is essential for sustainable development of the globe. Every responsible citizen should stand by the three billion youth of the world who are restless with the hope that youth can do it, nations can do it, and the world can do it", for making prosperity and peace of the world a reality." APJ Abdul Kalam, 8th convocation address of Nirma University of science and technology, Ahamdabad on 12th Oct, 2010.

Focus on Strategies for Higher Education

Value oriented Education-Education is extremely necessary for man. It leads to self-enlightenment and self-realization. Milton defines values as an enduring belief that a specific mode of conduct or end-state of existence is presently or socially preferable to an opposite or converse mode of conduct or end state of existence. The values are determinants of virtually all kinds of human behaviour that are known social behaviour. Value oriented education is now a days becoming a well—liked theme in the field of higher education. The loss of moral and social values among students is creating a conflict in the world. The factors leading to the loss of moral values may be enumerated as poverty, lack of faith in religious spirit, denominational religious practice in excessive form, unemployment, disintegrating tendencies, exploitation of nature, craze for money power and post, high aspirations, broken families, evil social customs dowry, low standard of living, cruel activities, recreational technologies such as cinema, T.V. computer etc. population growth and many others. Besides these adverse factors we have already dealt with so many heinous crimes, cruelties leading to craze for developing money –culture, noise-culture etc. which destroy our peace of mind and given rise to unwanted human uncultured. Cultural improvement requires real religious values which may be termed as essentials of different religious of the world. Value oriented education is more teacher and environment based the text books or ethical syllabus based. It is more awakening and informing. Values bring quality and meaning to life. It gives a person his individuality and character. Value oriented education helps in developing character, good behaviour, moral truthfulness, self discipline, kindness and love for all. Importing value to students is responsibility of parents, teachers and educational institutions etc. parents and teachers have direct concern with the education can make to the harmonization of valuable traditions and new values and the problems arising out of it.

Education can contribute significantly to harmonize valuable traditions and new values and the problems arising out of it. In this regard success lies in teacher's concern with the contribution education can make to such harmonization. Social and cultural traditions play a very significant part in the socialization of the youngsters including their cultural refinement. It is the role of education to promote and facilitate effective communication in society. Social and cultural traditions provide the purpose, meaning or rationale of life to the people.

Sri Aurobindo's concept of Integral Education consists primarily in developing the soul culture, which can given rise to the development of the integrated personality. Indira Sen rightly observes, "Integral growth of human personality implies the development of the rational, emotional as well as the volitional aspects of personality is developed'. Rishi's remark's that 'in the economy of man mental nature rests upon the moral, and the education of the intellect divorced from the perception of the moral, and emotional nature is injurious to human progress."

The campaign for value-oriented education has inspired several educationists and teachers in the field of school or college education and they have given various kinds of suggestion. Prof. Kalra, for example, says that at the primary level exemplary behaviour of the teacher is the most important feature together with the imparting of religious values, which must start with the Morning Prayer in the school. He firmly holds that "values are acquired by examples and they are imbibed by what we do, not by what we say to do'. The integration of modern and Indian classical values is possible by recognizing that scientific temper feeling of equality, economic justice, freedom and secularism can be included very well. The Indian values system underlines spiritual approach towards one life, generosity, tolerance anti-extremist attitude towards all problems of life and the concepts of four Varnas (in the original sense) and four Purusarthas as they signify the totaliy of view of Indian thought and also the qualities of human behaviour. In order to remove the social imbalance the society must not be far away from nature and giganticisms of modern technology must be minimized so that man may remain master of the machine. Prof. N.K. Dutt says that "In the self exploratory period of adolescence, the individual is in search of a hero from his immediate environment with whom he identifies (himself) and imbibes his values and character through the process of symbiosis formal teaching and discussions become relevant only when some good example is available to the youth".

Knowledge seeking and knowledge based education –Knowledge might be expected to imply strong support for and confidence in higher education institution. This apparent knowledge paradox may be explained by considering the more utility oriented conception of knowledge. Higher education growth makes an important background for more forceful and active presence of the state in higher education policy and management of the higher education system.

Gibbson *et al.* (1994) have given one of the most sweeping and widely known statements about the widening concept of knowledge in their book *The New production of knowledge.* They argue that a new form of knowledge production, "…a distinct set of cognitive and social practices is beginning to emerge" (Gibbsons *et al.* 1994, p. 3). The concept of knowledge is vague and ambiguous, definitions of the of the concept tend to vary according to what aspect of knowledge is emphasized. Broadly speaking, one finds one category of definitions that focuses on knowledge as some kind of outcome. This is the case of Deniel Bell's well-known definitions of knowledge as "a set of organized statements of fact or ideas" (Bell 1973, p. 41). What we call "Practical knowledge ", a concept that focuses on getting things made or done, shares the same characteristic, In general what we labeled 'utility oriented' knowledge also belongs to this category of knowledge. As a contrast there is a definition that focuses on knowledge as procedure. Cetina's concept of 'epistemic cultures distinguishes between cultures on the bases of process, or on how epistemic cultures make knowledge' in different ways (Knorr Cetina, 1999).

A number of frequently used pairs of concepts in the literature reflects this shared underlying distinction between knowledge as outcome and knowledge as procedure, such as 'theoretical' and 'practical' knowledge, a 'cultural' and 'utilitarian' purpose for basic research and higher education (Kogan *et al.* 2000), 'applied' and 'pure' research modes (Becher 1989).

The widening concept of knowledge cannot be taken to mean that 'we are being invaded' as had been around for a long time. It is for instance no novelty that result oriented knowledge exists in academia (e.g. law, medicine, and engineering etc. and applied science), however, its role and status in academia has changed. This change is visible in a number of ways. The process of justifying academia has changed, and new forms of organizing and funding research have emerged. Visible signs of this are the emergence of research parks, increased emphasis on externally funded research and the proliferation of thematic cross-disciplinary research centers. At the same time the positivist belief in scientific method, in knowledge as procedure has weakened as illustrated by Paul Feuerabend's thesis about "anything goes" (Feyerabend 1988 and Latour and Woolgar 1986). Mary Henkel (2000) in her study, points out that changes at the level of individual behaviour are for less marked than ideological and formal organizational changes. This finding was supported by the other nation studies in the three nation comparative project of which Henkel's study was a part (Kogan *et al.*, 2000), the mode of knowledge production is new, was to point out the aspects that only seem to be new and the ones that have not changed not much.

Gibbsons *et al.* (1994) and Gross *et al.* (1996) focuses on a development that they consider a general phenomenon which is affecting all academic research across the disciplines. Gibbsons and his collaborators focus on a general movement, one mode of knowledge production to another from an apparently descriptive position, but according to critics like Ziman (1996), it is also an implicit post-modern vision, a normative statement in favour of the same movement.

Knorr Cetina's book on 'epistemic cultures' seeks to demonstrate the diversity of the epistemic cultures of academic disciplines and the ways in which they make knowledge through a comparison of high energy physics and molecular biology. She claims that the diversity reveals the fragmentation of contemporary science: '...a whole landscape of independent epistemic monopolies producing vastly different products' (Knorr Cetina 1999, p. 4). whereas science traditionally has been regarded as an inner directed, intellectually self- propelled enterprise that has 'spoken' to society, it now increasingly finds itself integrated in society, embedded in a context that increasingly 'speaks back' to science. The process whereby this happens is extremely complex, as are its implications.

For example, the transition of higher education from an elite class to a mass system in North America, Europe and elsewhere, meant that a system that for centuries catered to very small fraction of the population in the matter of Research has experienced a similar growth, which means that employers—private companies, organizations and public enterprises—increasingly need research in order to do their job properly.

According to UNESCO, 'higher education is no longer a luxury; it is essential to national, social and economic development'. The quest to achieve Education for All (EFA) is fundamentally about assuring that children, youth and adults gain knowledge and skills they need to better their lives and to play a role in building more peaceful and equitable societies. This is why focusing on quality is an imperative for achieving EFA. As many societies strive universalize basic education, they face the momentous challenge of providing conditions where genuine learning can take place for each and every learner. Quality must be seen in light of how societies define the purpose of education (E.F.A., Global monitoring Report, 2005).

UNESCO report (2006) report, the need for international education will increase from 1.8 million international students in 2000 to 7.2 million international students in 2005. This rise creates huge challenges as well as opportunities. The or rising demand for higher education represented by an increase from 100.8 million tertiary students worldwide in 2000 to 173.5 million in 2009. The higher education sector has undergone major changes throughout the world which led to increased competition for institution in this sector (Kirp, 2003; Maringe and Gibbs, 2009).

A multitude of interconnected problems that India faces in its higher education system; in a summary ad particularly incisive diagnostic; and through analysis of the situation describes both the scope and challenges:

> "Higher education in India suffers from several systematic deficiencies. As a result, it continues to provide graduates that are unemployable despite emerging shortages of skilled man power in an increasing number of sectors. The standards of academic research are low and declining. Some of problems of the Indian higher education, such as the unwieldy affiliating system, inflexible academic structure, uneven capacity across various subjects, eroding autonomy of academic institutions, and the low level of public funding are well known. Many other concerns relating to the dysfunctional regulatory environment, the accreditation system that has low coverage and no consequences, absence, incentives for performing well and the unjust public funding policies are not well recognized".

For realization of India's extraordinary potential and aspirations for economic and technological development. Because, of this potential and its implications for individual advancement, there is an extraordinary demand for higher education among Indian youths.

Tertiary education is critical for the construction of knowledge economies. India currently produces a solid core of knowledge workers in tertiary and scientific and technical education, although the country needs to do more to create a longer cadre of educated and agile workers who can adapt and use knowledge. ....Measures are also needed to enhance the quality and relevance of higher education so that the education system is more demand driven quality conscious, and forward looking, especially to retain higher qualified people and meet the new and emerging needs of the economy (*ibid.*, xi-xii.) The knowledge based educational system is imposing an additional challenge to the educational system in India.

Never before higher education in India has emerged as a major force in building a knowledge society with inclusive growth and achieving development goals. Higher education has become a vital input for general, public good' and because it is a critical imperative for all levels of education. Higher education not only is the basis for generation of new knowledge, technology and skills through research, innovation and creativity but also facilitator for achieving "knowledge society with inclusive growth and hence has become a matter of great responsibility of all governments.

A qualitative and progressive higher education system will definitely bring quality of nation's life. Therefore, tomorrow's societies will be knowledge societies. Universities will have to pay a great role in shaping the future of tomorrow's societies.

Need of Life-Centered and Skill Centered Education

Skilled human capital and knowledge resource are two of the most— important factors for upgrading national competitive advantage. In this context, it is noteworthy that government has started a national skill development mission to fulfill the growing need for skilled people and has set a target for 500 million skilled people by the year 2022. (President of India Shrimati Pratibha Patil, 8th Annual convocation of Tripura University, 25 Sep. 2010).

All the young people constitute a significant part of the population in India; there is a growing need to integrate them with mainstream development of the nation. There is also need a strong relation to the education with the sensible aspect of life where a student can be skillfully made responsible for his or her behaviour or actions. Life entered Education is the right type of training and skills can be enhanced via life skills paradigm.

Life-skills are defined as the abilities for adaptive and positive behaviours that enable individuals to deal effectively with the demands and challenges of everyday life. Life skills contribute a continuum of knowledge and aptitudes that are necessary for a person to function independently and to avoid interruptions of the employment experience (Brotin, 1989). Life skills include self-development, interpersonal and family relationship development, communication skills, job and financial skills development, decision making, time management stress and anger management and the list go on.

All over the world nations are confronted with unparalleled challenges: the pressing need for rapid material advancement in the developing countries of the Third World and the rising incidence of psychological disturbances, crime and violence in the modern industrial nations of the West. Education is regarded as one of the key elements, if not the key, to the development of society, and, therefore, as an instrument for meeting these challenges. But it is now becoming apparent that the present educational system is unable of playing this role efficiently, because it is actually a source of these problems. The system itself needs to be changed so as to generate the solutions rather than contributing to the causes.

The present educational system is composed of two different strands which derive from different origins: the first, pure abstract knowledge in various fields of thought which is derived from the European tradition of liberal education for upper class gentlemen and the second, practical knowledge and technical skills relating to material objects and processes which emerged as a result of the recent industrial and technological revolutions. This system suffers from two major deficiencies: it divides knowledge into various separate subjects and disciplines, thereby making it partial and disconnected; and it divorces knowledge from real life, thereby making it abstract and unrelated to living. With the emergence of each new subject, knowledge became more detailed and study more specialized. The removal of traditional barriers to freedom of thought enabled mind to pursue each line of enquiry to its farthest ends. The development of new instruments of observation made possible the detailed analysis of physical facts which is the basis of modern science. These trends stimulated many fold the amassing of facts and information and the formulation of abstract theories and concepts to explain them.

The body of knowledge called modern science is the product of mind's division of existence into numerous separate fields of study and its one-dimensional investigation of each field. At the same time there has been a progressive withdrawal of the observer from the field of observation into the laboratory, a rapid development of theories and concepts, and a growing tendency to view life in terms of abstract thought rather than through direct observation. The result has been a fragmentation of knowledge and thought of knowledge from life. There is now a general consensus that the division of the study of social problems by different academic disciplines separated from one another by rigid theoretical and professional barriers is a major obstacle to the generation of effective solutions. To compensate for this inherent structural deficiency, a greater emphasis is being placed on interdisciplinary and inter-professional research on the problems of development.

Interdisciplinary study can mitigate some of the greater ills of specialization. They can prevent the creation of more planners who view development solely in terms of capital and technology ignoring the impact of political organization, education, social values and culture. They can provide technologists who become development administrators with an awareness of the consequences of rapid technological change on society and the environment. They can help future managers appreciate the political, social and cultural factors which influence the expansion of commerce and industry. They can foster the creation of more inclusive development strategies in place of one-sided approaches.

But a mere modification of the existing system to emphasize interdisciplinary studies, while welcome in itself, will not be sufficient to overcome the deficiencies of the present system or to resolve the most pressing social problems of developed and developing nations. Studies made from the multiple viewpoints of many separate disciplines instead of from only one discipline are still based on a fragmented approach without a real centre of reference. At most they can generate an awareness of the many aspects and proportions of social problems. They cannot unite these many diverse aspects in a single integral vision of the whole. At best a multidisciplinary approach can foster greater coordination among the various agencies involved in implementation. It cannot produce strategies which are harmoniously integrated with the present life of the society and designed to release its energies for development.

The basic limitation of an interdisciplinary approach is that it abandons the old centre of vision which is limited to the theoretical framework of a single specialized field without creating a new centre which is capable of integrating the divergent viewpoints of various disciplines.

Integrated Life-Centered Approach

The basis of this new approach is to take life itself as the center of perspective and to study it as an integral whole, rather than dividing the subject into specialized disciplines and abstracting it from its living context which destroys a vision of the whole and makes it extraneous to life. The aim should be to discover the common principles and processes which govern change in all fields of life, rather than constructing partial and limited theories to explain change in each different field. These principles and processes constitute the basic concepts of the Science of the Development of Life.

Each of the sciences of social life has identified basic laws or characteristic patterns of activity in their respective fields of enquiry. These laws are various expressions of universal principles which govern man's social existence, each law focusing on one dimension of social life which is integral. So long as social scientists view life from the different perspectives of their own disciplines, it is not possible to piece together the enormous number of inter-dependent factors to create an integral vision of the whole and a true view of interrelationships. For that, the partial laws and theories of each discipline must themselves be replaced by the more original principles of which they are all expressions.

Knowledge of Life Skills

Knowledge becomes effective in life only when it is expressed by the individual through his personality in his outer behaviour. The ability to express knowledge in life depends on the life skills and capacities which the individual possesses. In addition to imparting knowledge of the principles and processes of life, a life-centered education should also impart knowledge of the life skills and capacities necessary for translating knowledge into achievement. These skills are normally acquired subconsciously as an inheritance from the previous generation and through life experience, they are not taught in schools. The skill itself cannot be transferred through pure mental education, but a knowledge of the importance of these skills and their role in life can and should be taught.

There are many skills and capacities necessary for survival. The most important are the capacity for decision-making, a sense of responsibility for one's own life, the capacity to organize, the capacity to convert resources (potentials) into benefits (actualities) in one's own life, resourcefulness, patience, endurance, tolerance, accommodation, etc. As the student learns the importance of harmony and other life requirements for any lasting social achievement, he can learn the importance of essential human capacities. This aspect of life-centered education may be termed education of personality.

Identified Life Skills

World Health Organization (WHO, 1993) mentions that life- skills consists of 10 skills 15 points and divides the intelligence behaviour into three types as follows:

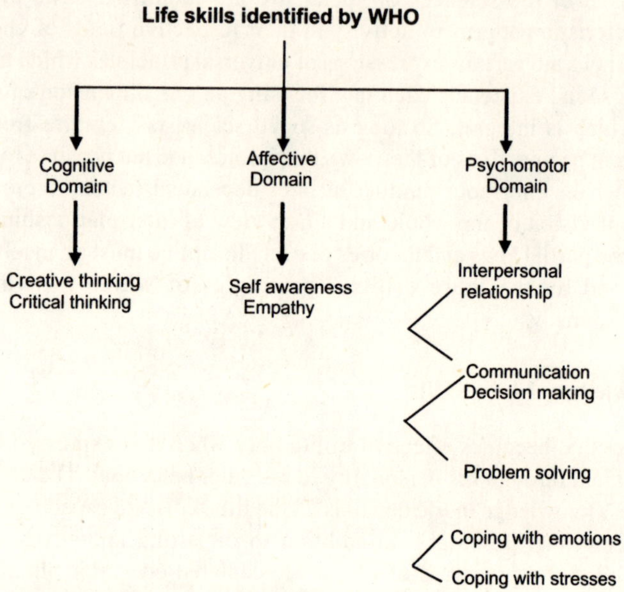

Fig. 11.1: Life Skills Identified by WHO

Cognitive Domain

It consists creative thinking (means the broadened thinking on original or innovative or artistic work etc.) and critical thinking (means the deliberation thinking while analyze any situational problem).

Affective Domain

Two life skills important in this domain are self awareness (means finding and understanding good or bad points of oneself) and empathy (means imaginative and spontaneous projection of ones self into an object or being, leading to sympathetic understanding or vivid experience of events witnessed.

Psychomotor Domain

It emphasizes three pairs of life skills where the first pair consists of interpersonal relationship which means social responsibility and communication means students can talk, speak and can use a body language for communication about what one feels. The second pair consists of decision-making which means that a final decision has been taken by the individual. In problem solving individual also selects, evaluates and decision-making is a process which occurs during problem solving. But not all decision-making is part of problem solving. It is therefore, presented as a separate thinking skill.

The third pair is concerned with coping with emotions and stress which means the students can evaluate emotion and its influence for self behaviour. They can react suitably and known the causes of stress and can handle emotions in a positive manner, know how to keep off problem and work constructively for stress.

Accordingly to UNICEF (2002) there is no definite list of life skills. Different life skills can emerge according to the time, situation, persons and local conditions prevalent under consideration.

Practical Approach on use of life skills: Life skills paradigm identifies significant life skills that can be used in a specific way to overcome the problems of life of an individual. Various checklists, inventories, training session or work shops etc. based on life skills training programmed can be used under life skills paradigm for enhancing the different life skills.

Knowledge Management for Higher Education: knowledge management principles recognize that it is important for organizations to know what they know. All institutions internally store, access and deliver knowledge in some manners. "Almost any institution in this century will make reference to the capturing of knowledge, the sharing of and the delivery of knowledge from faculty to students" explains Stevenson. However, knowledge management need much more, giving beyond the interest of knowledge industry of colleges and universities. In the EDUCAUSE: Leadership Strategies Volume entitled Information Alchemy: the Art and Science of knowledge management, Bembon explains that, K.M. involves the discovery and capture of knowledge, the filtering and arrangement—of this knowledge, and the value derived from shaving and using this knowledge management the organization (2001, p. XIV).

Higher education institutions have "significant opportunities to apply knowledge management practices to support every part of their mission", explains Kidwell *et al.* (2001, p. 24). "Knowledge management should not strike higher education institutions as a radically new idea; rather it is a new spin on their raison d'etre" (p. 24). The problem is that it is such a "wide open area of study that it is difficult to understand the implications of knowledge management for an educational setting" (Thorn, 2001, p. 25). This digest offers a basic introduction to the potential of KM for higher education.

"Knowledge Management (KM) is an effort to increase useful knowledge within the organization. Ways to do this include encouraging communication, offering opportunities to learn, and promoting the sharing of appropriate knowledge artifacts." This proposition is supported by:

- New process specific to the management of knowledge
- Organizational structures that create accountability for KM
- Applications that support km processes
- Enabling technologies

Knowledge management in education is the collection of processes that govern the creation, dissemination and utilization of knowledge. In one form or another, knowledge management has been around for a very long time. Practitioners have included philosophers, priests, teachers, politicians, scribes, Liberians etc., Knowledge management is not "A technology thing" or a "Computer thing" if we accept the premise that Knowledge management is concerned with the entire process of discovery and creation of knowledge then we are strongly driven to accept that Knowledge management is much more than a "Technology thing" and that elements of it exist in each of one Jobs. Knowledge management comprises a range of practices used by organizations to identify, create, represent and distribute knowledge. It has been an established discipline since 1995 with a body of university courses and both professional and academic journals dedicated to it. Knowledge management is frequently linked to the idea of the learning organization. Knowledge management refers to a range of practices used by organizations to identify the higher levels of innovations in education. The sharing of knowledge in industry, colleges, universities and, almost any institution in this country will make reference to the capturing of knowledge.

Expansion of Higher Education in India

The success stories of 'green revolution', 'space technology', 'nuclear energy' and 'information technology superiority India has achieved'-we owe these all to the higher education system as it evolved during 60 years of India's independence. It cannot be denied that it is Indian higher education system that to a significant extent has contributed to India rising to become the World's second fastest growing economy, the World's third largest economy, fastest growing mobile phone market, owner of the largest bandwidth capacity and contributing second largest portion of scientists and engineers in the world.

Expansion with Equity

India has experienced appreciable growth in the number of institutions of higher education during last six decades and particularly since 1990. This growth has already been because of expansion of number of State Universities and institutions deemed to be Universities. The period since 1990 has also seen the emergence of private Universities. The expansion of central universities has rather been slow and skewed in terms of regional distribution. It also mentioned that a significant majority of Universities, particularly managed by the state governments ate affiliating in nature. Given the current number of universities in the country the burden of affiliating colleges per University is unmanageably high and incongruous, in some cases the number of colleges affiliated to a University runs as high as many hundreds. Thus despite appreciable growth in number of universities there is scope rather need for further expansion in the number of universities and also colleges.

Inclusiveness and Equality

The participants in the Diversity, Inclusiveness, and Inequality track represented a great deal of diversity themselves and included faculty and students from a rich variety of research institutions, private liberal arts colleges, and community colleges. While participants engaged issues and strategies in each of the three substantive area—diversity, inclusiveness, and inequality in education (DIIE)—the bulk of our conversations focused on diversity and inequality.

Quality and Excellence

Ensuring quality education demands structural and institutional reforms in addition to committing enhanced financial resources. Imparting quality education would entail better infrastructure; greater use of ICT; teaching and learning in smaller groups; granting self-sufficiency to the faculty, department and individual teachers. But more than that, imparting quality education requires **'faculty development'** or what many call **'faculty recharge programmes'** so that the faculty does not go stale, it retains its vibrancy and dynamism in doing research, in learning, and innovating and in devising new methods of teaching.

In the modern technological world quality education has become a necessity. Governments all over the world are appointing committees and commissions to bring in excellence in education. Curricular are being revised and improved to include more and more relevant knowledge in the curricula of schools and colleges.

Academic and Administrative Reforms

Unlike expansion, equity/inclusiveness and quality/excellence, where efforts are in making, the policies concerning reforms in the arena of academics, administration and governance are already well formulated and publicity announced.

While these recommendations about credit system, semester system, more of international assessment and less written examination component, teachers evaluation by students, inter-institutional mobility etc. have been generally accepted, quite a few of them have not been implemented and operationalized as yet. Some of these have been tried and failed while some others have been implemented on selective basis. As a result there is a lot of institutional variations in admission, examination, faculty and governance related practices

It also explains about the Knowledge management and types of Knowledge management and their trends and new innovations of Knowledge management in current education scenario. Educational trends and tasks are towards more learner- centered materials. In response to these trends, colleges and universities are offering new courses at a distance and forms traditional delivery. The effort to share the most recent understandings about Knowledge management in education is the changing roles and challenges for higher education. The increased productivity required by faculty are driving forces for the development of more diverse and efficient teaching method.

Knowledge management education is the process of constructively using the information and knowledge that is inherent to any organization be it a school university or multinational company.

Concept of Knowledge Management in Education

- Education for Knowledge
- Education for Information
- Education for Skills
- Education for Employment
- Education for Livelihood
- Education for Empowerment
- Education for Social and National Development

Key Tasks Involved in Education for Knowledge Management

A. Micro-Level Management of Tasks

- Course structuring and study material preparation
- Distribution and presentation of study materials
- Communication between educational actors (student-faculty, student-student)
- Performing instructional assignments, either alone or group-based
- Performance assessment

B. Macro-Level Management of Tasks

- Organisation of the whole educational process
- Organising and managing information and knowledge flows within the educational organisation
- Keeping track of performance of students, faculty, courses, curriculum, and of the (allocation of) available knowledge resources
- Monitoring results in terms of goals and standards
- Dynamic changing of the educational programme as feedback to discrepancies between goals and standards and obtained performance results.

Knowledge Management Focus

"The focus on knowledge management is on 'doing the right thing' instead of doing things right'. It provides a framework within which the organization views all its processes as knowledge processes and all business processes involve creation, dissemination and application of knowledge towards organizational sustenance and survival".

Knowledge Types

It contains two types these are:

- Explicit knowledge
- Tacit knowledge

Explicit Knowledge

- Objective, rational, technical
- Easily documented
- Easily transferred/taught/learned

Tacit Knowledge

- Subjective, cognitive, experiential learning
- Hard to document
- Hard to transfer/teach/learn
- Involves a lot of human interpretation

Knowledge Management Process

The process of Knowledge Management applicable to schools, colleges and universities. Some would argue that sharing knowledge is their reason of being. If that is the case, then the higher education sector should be replete with examples of institutions that leverage knowledge to spur innovation, improve services, or achieve operational excellence. However, although some examples exist, they are the exception rather than the rule. Knowledge Management is not a new field, and experiments are beginning to mature in higher education.

New Trends in Knowledge Management

Several trends will shape the field of knowledge management in the not-too distant future (even now):

- Emerging technology solutions
- The convergence of knowledge management with e-business
- The movement from limited knowledge management projects to more enterprise wide projects
- Increasing use of knowledge management to enhance innovation
- Increasing use of tacit knowledge (rather than explicit knowledge).

Knowledge management refers to a range of practices used by organizations to identify the higher levels of innovations in education. The sharing of knowledge in industry, colleges, universities and, almost any institution in this country will make reference to the capturing of knowledge. By developing the knowledge management, the nation's economy increases and can compete in the global scenario.

Use of Technology in Higher Education as Service-Learning Strategies

Science and Technology will increasingly influence the course of human civilization and hold the key to economic growth and social development.

Certainly higher education has begun to make greater use of information technology, especially on the non-instructional side of the enterprise—administrative functions in particular. The application of information technology to instruction, however, is still in its early stages, even though states and institutions have begun to invest considerable sums to incorporate its use into courses and academic programmes. Until now, the main focus on technology has been to tap into its potential to enhance the quality of education. More and more courses incorporate tools such as e-mail or web resources, and a small but growing number use even more advanced techniques such as reproduction and multimedia, which expand and diversify the pedagogy traditionally relied upon by higher education. This use of information technology in higher education is, however, almost always an add-on to the traditional delivery system with the primary purpose of enhancing the educational experience. As such, it tends to drive up costs, both for the technology itself and the increased time demands on both faculty and highly skilled technical staff.

Widespread use of technology is changing the way we work, learn, and communicate-even the way we carry out our regular, daily activities. In higher education, technology has had a dramatic impact on teaching and learning, including service-learning experiences. Service-learning classes and activities can be augmented through the use of technology to provide more effective experiences for faculty, students and community participants. With their ready access to new technologies, higher educational institutions are well-positioned to take advantage of rapid changes in the field.

There are a number of ways that technology can enhance service-learning programmes while conserving programme resources:

- *Programme management*: Databases can help programme staff to track student placements, community partner contact information and the academic calendar.

- *Community partner participation*: A well-publicized web site can describe the service-learning programmes, provide easy access to forms for registering a community project and highlight stories of positive community partner experiences.
- *Curricular tools*: Online modules and case studies can enhance classroom and community-based learning.
- *Community service*: Meaningful community service doesn"t necessarily have to involve regular or ongoing face-to-face contact between student and community partner
- *Reflection*: Electronic discussion groups can enable students across different service-learning sites to regularly communicate, share their experiences and respond to reflective questions posed by faculty and one another.
- *Programme evaluation:* For example, online surveys can enable students and community partners to respond to questions about their experiences and the impact of the programme. Databases can facilitate the tracking and storage of programme evaluation information.

One goal of service-learning is to *create* community, therefore some skeptics question the use of technology in service-learning. They focus on the potential for separation and disconnectedness that can result from over-reliance or sole reliance on high skill. Technology will certainly never be able to replace human interaction and exchange, which is at the core of service-learning experiences and essential to the development of trust between campus and community. These face-to-face exchanges are critical to sustaining service-learning partnerships. In fact, "community" and "technology" should not be considered mutually exclusive events—one may be used to enhance the other. Certain sub-populations, such as shy and introverted individuals, may actually be more inclined to participate in a "virtual" community than a "physical" community. Technology can engage learners with communities in a dynamic relationship.

There are a number of challenges to using technology in service-learning. Many of us are not facile with technology or the range of applications currently available. Rapidly evolving technology makes it nearly impossible keep up with the latest technological advances. The differential access to technology among faculty, learners and community partners can pose a challenge. Inadequate resources (i.e., time, money and people) to continually update technology (i.e., updating web pages) can be a major

Use of E-learning: E-learning is the expression broadly used to describe a "instructional content or learning experience delivered or enabled by electronic technologies" (Ong and Wang, 2004).

Laurillard (2006) has defined e- learning as the use of any of the new technologies or applications in the science of learning or learners support. It is important because e-learning can make a significant difference to how learners learn, how quickly they master a skill, how easy it to study, and equally important—how much they enjoy learning. E-learning includes all forms of electronically supported learning and teaching including Etechd. The information and communication system, whether networked learning or not, serve as specific media to implement the learning processThe term will still most likely be utilized to reference out-of-classroom and in-classroom educational experiences via technology, even as advances continue in regard to devices and curriculum. Abbreviations like CBT (*Computer-Based Training*), IBT (*Internet-Based Training*) or WBT (*Web-Based Training*) have been used as synonyms to e-learning.

E-learning is the computer and network-enabled transfer of skills and knowledge. E-learning applications and processes include Web-based learning, computer-based learning, virtual learning opportunities and digital collaboration. Content is delivered via the Internet, intranet/ extranet, audio or video tape, satellite TV, and CD-ROM. It can be self-paced or instructor-led and includes media in the form of text, image, animation, streaming video and audio.

It is commonly thought that new technologies can strongly help in education. In young ages especially, children can use the huge interactivity of new media, and develop their skills, knowledge, perception of the world, under their parents monitoring, of course. Many proponents of e-learning believe that everyone must be equipped with basic knowledge in technology, as well as use it as a medium to reach a particular goal.

Higher Education

By 2006, 3.5 million students were participating in on-line learning at institutions of higher education in the United States. According to the Sloan Foundation reports, there has been an increase of around 12—14 per cent per year on average in enrollments for fully online learning over the five years 2004—2009 in the US post-secondary system, compared with an average of approximately 2 per cent increase per year in enrollments overall. Allen and Seaman (2009) claim that almost a quarter of all students in post-secondary education were taking fully online courses in 2008, and a report by Ambient Insight Research suggests that in 2009, 44 per cent of post-secondary students in the USA were taking some or all of their courses online, and projected that this figure would rise to 81 per cent by 2014.

In higher education especially, the increasing tendency is to create a Virtual learning environment (VLE) (which is sometimes combined with a Management Information System (MIS) to create a Managed Learning Environment in which all aspects of a course are handled through a consistent user interface standard throughout the institution. A growing number of physical universities, as well as newer online-only colleges, have begun to offer a select set of academic and certificate programmes via the Internet at a wide range of levels and in a wide range of disciplines. While some programmes require students to attend some campus classes or orientations, many are delivered completely online. In addition, several universities offer online student support services, such as online advising and registration, e-counseling, online textbook purchase, student governments and student newspapers.

E-Learning can also refer to educational web sites such as those offering learning scenarios, worksheets and interactive exercises for children. The term is also used extensively in the business sector where it generally refers to cost-effective online training.

The recent trend in the E-Learning sector is screen casting. There are many screen casting tools available but the latest buzz is all about the web based screen casting tools which allow the users to create screen casts directly from their browser and make the video available online so that the viewers can stream the video directly. The advantage of such tools is that it gives the presenter the ability to show his ideas and flow of thoughts rather than simply explain them, which may be more confusing when delivered via simple text instructions. With the combination of video and audio, the expert can mimic the one on one experience of the classroom and deliver clear, complete instructions. From the learner's point of view this provides the ability to pause and rewind and gives the learner the advantage of moving at their own pace, something a classroom cannot always offer.

Research on the use of video in lessons is preliminary, but early results show an increased retention and better results when video is used in a lesson. Creating a systematic video development method holds promise for creating video models that positively impact student learning.

Communication Technologies Used in E-Learning

Communication technologies are generally categorized as asynchronous or synchronous. *Asynchronous* activities use technologies such a blogs, wikis, and discussion boards. The idea here is that participants may engage in the exchange of ideas or information without the dependency of other participant's involvement at the same time. Electronic mail (Email) is also asynchronous in that mail can be sent or received without having both the participants' involvement at the same time. Asynchronous learning also gives students the ability to work at their own pace. This is particularly beneficial for students who have health problems or have child care responsibilities and regularly leaving the home to attend lectures is difficult. They have the opportunity to complete their work in a low stress environment and within a more flexible timeframe.

Synchronous activities involve the exchange of ideas and information with one or more participants during the same period of time. A face to face discussion is an example of synchronous communications. In an e-learning learning environment, an example of synchronous communications would be a Skype conversation or a chat room where everyone is online and working collaborativelly at the same time. *Synchronous* activities occur with all participants joining in at once, as with an online chat session or a virtual classroom or meeting.

Virtual classrooms and meetings can often use a mix of communication technologies. Participants in a virtual classroom use icons called emoticons to communicate feelings and responses to questions or statements. Students are able to 'write on the board' and even share their desktop, when given rights by the teacher. Other communication technologies available in a virtual classroom include text notes, microphone rights, and breakout sessions. Breakout sessions allow the participants to work collaboratively in a small group setting to accomplish a task as well as allow the teacher to have private conversations with his or her students.

The virtual classroom also provides the opportunity for students to receive direct instruction from a qualified teacher in an interactive environment. Students have direct and immediate access to their instructor for instant feedback and direction. The virtual classroom also provides a structured schedule of classes, which can be helpful for students who may find the freedom of asynchronous learning to be overwhelming. The virtual classroom also provides a social learning environment that closely replicates the traditional "brick and mortar" classroom. Most virtual classroom applications provide a recording feature. Each class is recorded and stored on a server, which allows for instant playback of any class over the course of the school year. This can be extremely useful for students to review material and concepts for an upcoming exam. This also provides students with the opportunity to watch any class that they may have missed, so that they never have to fall behind. It also gives parents the ability to monitor any classroom to insure that they are satisfied with the education their child is receiving.

In *asynchronous* online courses, students proceed at their own pace. If they need to listen to a lecture a second time, or think about a question for awhile, they may do so without fearing that they will hold back the rest of the class. Through online courses, students can earn their diplomas more quickly, or repeat failed courses without the embarrassment of being in a class with younger students. Students also have access to an incredible variety of enrichment courses in online learning, and can participate in college courses, internships, sports, or work and still graduate with their class.

In many models, the writing community and the communication channels relate with the E-learning and the M-learning communities. Both the communities provide a general overview of the basic learning models and the activities required for the participants to join the learning sessions across the virtual classroom or even across standard classrooms enabled by technology. Many activities, essential for the learners in these environments, require frequent chat sessions in the form of virtual classrooms and/or blog meetings.

Such a complex set of technologies will make following kinds of impact on the experience of learning:

Cultural: Students are comfortable with E-learning methods, as they are similar to the forms of information search and communications methods they use in other parts of their lives.

Intellectual: Interactive technology offers a new mode of engagement with ideas via both material and social interactivity online.

Social: The reduction in social difference afforded by online networking fits with the idea that students should take greater responsibility for their own learning.

Practical: E-learning offers the ability to manage quality at scale, and share resources across networks. Its greater flexibility of provision in time and place make participation.

Use of M-learning: People in Asia and Europe are finding that their connectivity and computing needs can be met through mobile phone (Wagner, 2003). The learners need to share photos and news with classmate and teachers via the mobile phones. M-Learning provides an opportunity to get touch with the group of hard to reach learners.

Every student participates in mobile learning has equal opportunity to make quality presentations, communicate with faculty and access course materials without waiting for the campus (Quinn, 2006). Students have access to test and assignments and results.

Mobile phones use the wireless Internet to exchange voice massages, e-mail and web pages at anywhere and anytime. Since most students already carry mobile phones, most classes are already equipped. Portability, connectivity, simplicity and low cost make them valuable educational tools and running cost and text input speed restrict its uses.

Mobile phones e-mail produced learning as superior to desktop. e-mail mobile web and paper (Houser, 2002). In Singapore, courses, already to the people's convenience, they were planning to offer an entire distance education course through mobile phones even with limitations of tiny size of phones, less memory and screens (Ring, 2001).

Curriculum of Higher Education: Curriculum of Higher education requires a strong emphasis on effective design of educational programmes, curricula and learning environments. Curriculum design must include effective means of gauging student progress.

As per recommendations of NPE-1986 the system of education must be evaluated every five years but as a insider it is not done for more then a decade or two. So today education is looked at as service industry and teaching as a profession, therefore obviously it demands accountability, professionalism and transparency.

Evaluation system in higher education: Process of evaluation consists of collecting evidence and making judgment based on evidence. Performance evaluation is a necessary component of any examination system. The evaluation of students has been considered to play a pivotal role in the education system.

There are mainly two schemes of performance evaluation prevalent in the education system—first, in home examination system, where officiated or constituent institutions have full comfort over the evaluation process and second—centralized examination system conducted by an educational Board/Body/University. Both the practices have their own importance and usefulness.

The development system is very important for the growth of a society. For the education system to function satisfactory, continuous monitoring and corrective measures are very important. The education system should not compromise with quality and any cost. The stamp of quality can be obtained by an impartial evaluation through centralization/uniform examination system also. The education system should display robustness by reducing the possibility of manipulation in student evaluation. (R.C. Sobti and A. Bhandari, 2009, *University News*, New Delhi Vol. 47, No. 48).

Challenges and strategies in producing required number of qualified teachers is a big challenge for Higher Education. In the context of limited sources and increasing number of educational aspirants, meeting the requirement of more number of qualified teachers' demands for new flexible, cost effective, technology mediated modules and strategies without compromising the quality and standards. The quality teaching/learning modules, the methodology and evaluation for teacher education and training need to be learner friendly, facilitating for continuous training and up gradation of the knowledge and skills relevant to changing educational situation demands.

More than three decades ago and in his assessment of the roles of higher education the French professor of philosophy and the sixth Director General of UNESCO, Rene Maheu (1947) lamented and the problem with higher education institution is that they were not responding quickly enough and are not proactive to the changing context of the society and the globe. He suggested that it is necessary to regenerated higher education to cope with the changes affecting the society, and do this, we have to transform higher education to the new needs of the community and the individuals of the community and the individuals economically, socially and culturally. His view was similarly echoed later by the president of the club of Rome, Richard Diez- Hogchitner (1996) who said that "Education must not only be adapted to the needs of our age, it must also make real effort to look ahead some twenty five years".

Universities can be sources of new knowledge and innovative thinking. It is important that Universities have an environment sympathetic to and supportive of innovation. Success of our future generation depends on the ability to innovate and adapted the aim also has to be research and innovation that is of international standards. (President of India Shrimati Prativa Patil, 8th Annual Convocation of Tripura Universities 25 Sep. 2010).

Developmental Strategies aim at reforming higher education in independent, strong and objective analysis in independent, strong and objective analysis of ground reality. The central objective of the 11th plan is now focused on expansion of enrolment in higher education with inclusiveness, quality and relevant education and supported by necessary Academic Reforms in the University Academic Reforms in the University and college system in India. There are necessary that individual state and central government also take similar initiative in their respective state plan and develop policies to address the issue of increasing the enrolment rate, equal access to groups with lower access to higher education, issue of quality, relevant education and various academic reforms.

REFERENCES

Agarwal, Pawan (2006). Higher Education in India: The Need for Change. (ICIER) working. Indian Council for Research on International Economic Relations. New Delhi.

Bhatia, Karuna, Manaoj Kumar Dash (2010). A Comparative Analysis of Higher Education System of India with Other Countries. *American Journal of Scientific Research.* ISSN1450-223 Issue 12 137-152.

E-learning _Free Wikipedia.Internet.

Ivar, Bleikle and Haldor Byrkjeflot (2002). *Changing Knowledge Regimes: Universities in New Research Environment*. Higher Education. Kluwer Academic Publishers. 519-532.

Jaiswal, Vijoy and Priyanka Gupta (2010). E-Learning in Higher Education: Indian Perspective, *University News*, AIU New Delhi Vol. 48, No. 03, Ten–18-24.

Meena (2010). The Need for Life Centred Education via Skills Paradigm, *University News*, AIU, New Delhi, Vol. 48, No. 17, April 26-May 02.

Milan, Jonh H: Knowledge Management for Higher Education, ERIC Digent; Internet.

Parthiban, S. and William, B.D. Raja (2010). M. Learning: A Novel Avenue to Education; *University News*, AIU, New Delhi.

Patil, Prathiva Devsingh (2010). Education is the Process of Man Making; Covocation Address, 8 M Annual Convocation, Tripura Universities 25th Sep. 2010 *University News*, AIU New Delhi Vol. 48, No. 47 Nov. 22-28.

Peter, Michael. Higher Education, Development and Learning Community. Internet

Sarenena, D. Seifer and Tanis Vye Milanynuk (2005).The Use of Technology in Higher Education Service Learning. Community-Campus Partnership Health.Internet

Soni, Rashmi and M.S. Sodh (2009). Flexible Perception of Quality in Higher Education and Quality in the Light of Available Inputs and Priorities. *University New*, AIU, New Delhi. Vol. 47, No. 50, Dec. 14-20.

WHO (1993). Promoting Health Through schools. Reports of a WHO expert committee or comprehensive school Health Education and promotion, WHO, Technical Report Service 870, division of publishing Geneva 27, series Switzerland.

Contributors

Alberto Arenas, *Ph.D.,* is Associate Professor, specializes in the intersection between environmental and sustainability education with sociology of education and history of education. He was also a Fulbright-Hays Doctoral Fellow in Colombia. He is the author of over 60 publications and conference papers, and his manuscripts have been published in some of the leading educational journals and UNESCO-UNEVOC. Professor Arenas is a member of the Commission on Education and Communication (North America and the Caribbean Region) of the International Union for Conservation of Nature (IUCN), based in Gland, Switzerland, Scientific Committee of the 7th World Environmental Education Congress (Morocco). For the period 2013-2014, he was awarded a Fulbright Scholar Grant to do research in Mexico on environmental and sustainability education.

Debdulal Dutta Roy, *Ph.D.,* is Assistant Professor of Psychology Research Unit of the Indian Statistical Institute, Kolkata. He is the Executive Council member of the Indian Academy of Applied Psychology and member of the Editorial Board of the Journal of the Indian Academy of Applied Psychology. He is the division convener of the Psychological assessment of the National Academy of Psychology (NAOP). Dr. Dutta Roy is the member of the Board of Governing Council of Insurance Bureau of India (IIB). He is the Member, Advisory Board. Performing Arts Therapy center, Rabindra Bharati University, Kolkata; Member, Academic Council of the Calcutta Metropolitan Institute of Gerontology, Kolkata; Member, Academic Advisory Board of Jyotirmoy School of Business from November, 2010; Member of the Editorial Board of the 'Journal of Management Research in Emerging Economies of Dr. B.C. Roy Engineering College, Durgapore; Adjunct Faculty of Business School of Amrita Vishwa vidyapeetham.

Dharmarakshit Gautam is a doctoral scholar at National University of Educational Planning and Administration (NUEPA), New Delhi. His area of research encompasses various dimensions of global politics pertaining to sustainable education with the help of traditional as well as modern approaches.

Emon Nandi is a doctoral scholar at Zakir Husain Centre for Educational Studies, School of Social Sciences, Jawaharlal Nehru University and working within broader gamut of economics of Education.

Dr. Hafeez-ur-Rehman was Tenured Track Professor of Social Anthropology in the Department of Anthropology at Quaid-i-Azma University, Islamabad. He has been the Chairman of the Department of Anthropology for almost 10 years. He has published more than 87 research articles in journals of National and International repute and contributed several chapters in the books. His work on Saints and Shrines in Pakistan from anthropological perspective makes him distinguished from other contemporary scholars of this discipline. He has also participated and contributed papers in almost 43 countries at global level. Dr. Hafeez has supervised 18 PhD scholars, 64 M.Phil and more than 360 M.Sc. student of Anthropology. He is also involved in applied anthropology and has conducted several research studies (64 research projects) with various Organizations. His area of specialization is applied anthropology. He has worked as Principle Investigator/Link coordinator with several HEC-BC research projects.

Jayanti Basu, *Ph.D.*, is Professor in Department of Applied Psychology, University of Calcutta with about 27 years of teaching experience. Her areas of interest include clinical, health and social psychology. She has published about 100 papers in national and international journals, and few books. She has completed major projects on psychology of gender and neuropsychological aspects of old age. She has supervised about 18 Ph.D. students and is the Associate Editor of the Indian Journal of Applied Psychology. She is also a registered Psychoanalyst and member of many national and international academic bodies.

Dr. Saif Ullah Chaudhry did his Ph.D. in Anthropology from the Department of Anthropology at Quaid-i-Azam University, Islamabad. He is working as senior program officer in International Labor Organization (ILO) Islamabad. He has experience of participating in various National and International Conferences and contributed research papers. His area of specialization is Child Labor in cultural context. He is a young scholar with broad vision and innovative ideas.

Md. Amjad Kavesh is a Ph.D. scholar of Anthropology in the University of Sydney, Australia. He did his M.Phil in Anthropology from Quaid-i-Azam University, Islamabad. Md. Kavesh is regular contributor in various journals of National and International repute.

Mukund N. Bapat, *Ph.D.,* was the Professor at Regional Institute of Education, Bhopal, India. His area of interest zoomed over the pedagogical aspects of science education.

Sanat K. Ghosh, *Ph.D.,* is Professor of Education in Rabindrabharati University. As an adviser of BRAC and UNICEF, he carried out several projects in various nations centering round the issue of EFA. Professor Ghosh was also the former Director of Distance Education of Rabindrabharati University.

Saumen Chattopadhyay, *Ph.D.,* is Associate Professor of at Zakir Husain Centre for Educational Studies in School of Social Sciences of Jawaharlal Nehru University and specializes in economics of Education.

Sima Pal, *Ph.D.,* is Assistant Professor of Education in *Sir Ashutosh Mukhyopadhyaya* School of Educational Studies in Assam Central University, Silchar. She possesses almost a decade of post graduate teaching and research experience in Central University and has published several research articles. Her area of interest is Education of social groups in Northeast India.

Sreekala Edannur, *Ph.D.,* is Assistant Professor in faculty of Education, Pondicherry University. Dr. Sreekala possesses over a decade of post graduate teaching and research experience in Central Universities of India. She has published several research articles and books. She is currently working on an MHRD-UNICEF Project. She specializes in sociology of education and blended learning.

Yazali Josephine, *Ph.D.,* is Professor of National University of Educational Planning and Administration specializes in Economics of Education. Professionally trained in Educational Planning and Administration from IIEP (UNESCO), Paris, she obtained Post Graduate diploma in Developmental Administration from International University for Cooperation, Rome, Italy. Professor Yazali Conducted several impact research studies related to DPEP, Girls education and Incentive Programmes at School level, presented several research papers in the national and international organizations like UNESCO, Oxford etc. and published several research articles related to educational resource planning and management. She is currently working in the area of Globalization, Education and Poverty.